D1408873

Healing Circles: Grieving, Healing, and Bonding with Our Animal Companions

by Joy Davy, MS, LCPC, NCC

The cases presented here are composites with details changed, in order to protect the privacy of individuals.

Cover art by Andrea Mistretta.

Website: http://www.andreamistretta.com/

Dedication:

This book is dedicated to all the heroes in animals' lives: the rescuers and the adopters, the activists and the educators, all those who have reached out to heal an animal, and all those who have been healed by an animal. Keep on going, with your hearts open.

Introduction: How to Read this Book

You

You are an animal lover, picking up this book because you are grieving the loss of a cherished animal companion. Or perhaps you are deeply fascinated by the human-animal bond and would like to understand more about the profound connections we can form with our pets. I invite you to find comfort and company in these pages.

If you are grieving, you will find practical suggestions for dealing with your grief as well as examples of how other people have dealt with theirs. Read this book at your own pace. Read it in bits and pieces if you find that works best for you. As always, attend to your own emotions. This means: be aware of what you are feeling, without judging. Tune into your own needs. Crying can be cathartic, so if you find that parts of this book make you cry, that's not necessarily a bad thing.

Reading this book may be a solace and a help to you, as I certainly hope it will. Avail yourself of other support as well, by all means: pet loss hotlines, a pet grief support group, individual therapy with a professional counselor who understands pet grief, and any friends you have who will hear your story in a non-judging way. At the end of this book, you will find a resource list.

This Book

This is a book about two healing circles that exist between us and our companion animals.

The first healing circle is about how animals heal us emotionally, and how we heal them. As Helen Keller famously said, "Life is full of suffering. It is also full of the overcoming of it." Animals and people heal each other's suffering. A common bumper sticker you see these days has a big paw print, and reads: "Who rescued whom?" Animals who have been abandoned and abused are healed by the people who rescue them and commit themselves to the animals' care. They learn to trust and to feel safe again.

Companion animals everywhere heal people by keeping us company, giving us physical touch, a sense of play, a sense of purpose and being needed, by connecting us with the natural world, by being trustworthy and non-judging in a way that other people cannot be, and by some mysterious connection beyond words or explanation. In this book, as we explore grieving, healing, and bonding, the deeply meaningful connection between people and animals will continually come to the forefront. One of the best places to witness the human-animal bond is in pet grief support groups, where people share with others all that their animal friend has meant to them over time.

Humane societies, rescue groups, and sanctuaries have grown up everywhere to save neglected, abused and abandoned animals. At the same time, we now have not only guide dogs for the blind, but also animal assisted therapy such as that provided by emotional support dogs and equine therapy to treat Post Traumatic Stress Disorder, Anxiety, and a host of other forms of suffering in humans.

The second healing circle, centered within the first, is about our emotional cycle in the natural course of our animal-human relationship: bonding, grieving and healing. Grieving inevitably follows bonding. Grief is not shocking (although the circumstances of the loss may be). Grief is as natural and normal as the healing which follows it, and as natural and normal as the bonding—once again—that follows healing. It takes time and intention to build the bond, and the bond between an animal and his or her person is unique and intriguing to explore.

Just as the bond is unique, so is the grief when we are separated from our animal companions; the grief can overwhelm and surprise us with its ferocity. This grief is as real and as worthy of being honored as any other grief, but is often dismissed by others who don't understand or are uncomfortable with our (and their own) pain. Just as the bond took time and intention to build, so the grief takes time and intention (in the form of mourning) to heal. As we heal, we find ourselves changed.

Animals connect us with our compassion—for ourselves and for others. As we heal from the loss of an animal, we find that the connection that our animal made for us is still within us, a part of us.

Part One of this book will be of special interest to those currently grieving the loss of a very dear animal companion, and to those who have ever experienced that very deep grief.

Part Two explores how animals heal us, and how we heal them, and how we heal from pet grief.

Part Three is a look at the beautiful bond between people and their companion animals.

Part One: Grieving

The Nature of Grief

The Nature of Grief

Grief is different for all of us and in some ways the same for all of us.

Grief is natural. It is not an illness or a disorder. Loss is part of life, and your resistance to losing what you love is what creates your grief.

Grief is cumulative. Every new loss has the potential to stir up all the old losses, consciously or unconsciously. Acknowledging each loss helps you deal with further losses in life.

Grief has a life of its own. It cannot be rushed or suppressed; when you try to rush it or suppress it, it simply goes underground--only to come up later when you least expect it. When you don't acknowledge your grief and allow it expression, it tends to convert into a depression, an addiction or another illness.

Grief comes in waves. You can think you are "past it," only to find yourself hit with another "grief burst" that seems to come out of nowhere.

Grief takes its own time. It may never fully "resolve," but instead lessen to a point where it can integrate into the person you become.

Grief changes us. And that's okay.

The Classic Stages of Grief:

Elizabeth Kubler-Ross first brought awareness to the Stages of Grief that she observed when working with dying patients. Since her work was published, others have added in other stages, such as "guilt," and "yearning." These "stages" might better be called "elements," or some other name that does not apply a linear progression, because people don't go through these in a numerical fashion and then arrive neatly at the end. You could experience more than one stage at a time. You could find yourself moving through denial, anger and bargaining, and then cycling back to denial again. You could find that you don't experience one or more of these. For that reason, these pieces of grief are listed here with bullet points rather than numbers:

- **Denial**
- **Anger**
- **Bargaining**
- **Depression**
- **Guilt**
- **Yearning**
- **Acceptance**

Denial: This is when the situation seems surreal. "This can't be happening," you may think. When in denial, sometimes people don't see how sick their pet is; they may cling to hope that he will get better in spite of all evidence to the contrary. Bethany, who grew up with her golden retriever mix, said, "I never imagined my life without Arnie; somehow I thought he'd always be with me. I know that doesn't make sense, and that dogs don't live as long as people do. But I really never thought there'd be a time when he wouldn't be here. It feels like a terrible mistake has been made."

Anger: You may feel rage at God for "taking away" your pet. You may feel anger at your pet for "leaving." You may blame your vet or vet techs and later realize that this was not fair. (If that happens, it will make you and them feel better if you send a note or call and apologize.) You may lose patience randomly in a way that is not characteristic of you.

Bargaining: Margaret and John, a retired couple in their seventies, cannot bear losing their cat, Marvin, to cancer. They have emptied their savings account and borrowed money from friends to continue treatments for him, even though he is dying with no hope of recovery, and his quality of life is poor. "We'll do anything to save him," they say. "We would sell our house to pay his vet bills. Money doesn't matter. Only Marvin matters." Margaret and John cling to the hope that if they spend enough money, Marvin will be well.

Depression: Isolation; sleep disturbances; forgetting to eat (or eating too much); deep, mournful sighs; long bouts of crying; emotional numbness: these are some of the signs of depression while grieving. Barb looks at a photograph of Mona, her cat, on her refrigerator, and addresses it tearfully: "Why? Why are you gone? You are supposed to be here!"

Guilt: Guilt is thought to be part of Denial: you reflect on what you might have done differently, and if you had acted differently your pet would still be here (or so you reason), and that gives you a very small break from the intense pain that you feel because your pet is not here. But then you cycle back again to realizing that events unfolded the way they did, and your pet is, in fact, not here. People in pet grief groups have said they feel guilty because they didn't see the signs of an illness sooner, because they didn't check to see that the gate had been left open, because they should have made the decision to euthanize sooner, because they made the decision to euthanize too soon, because they should have spent more time playing with their pet when he or she was alive, and so on. We can always find something to feel guilty about if we try, and if there is nothing for us to feel guilty about, our grief seems to manufacture something. Know that this guilt, although it feels logical now, is more than likely not based on anything real.

Yearning: This is the intense longing to hold your pet, to feel the weight of your pet in your arms, to touch that fur once more. You may notice this yearning feeling to be especially strong about three months after the death of your pet.

Acceptance: The sadness is still there, but it is not as raw. Along with memories of the loss of your pet, you enjoy memories of your happy times together.

More about Grief and Guilt

The voice choking with pain releases the worst of it all: "and it's my own fault."

Guilt seems to be an integral part of grieving.

When grieving for an animal that we loved, we all seem to spend some time in a painful cell of guilt: "I should have taken him to the vet sooner." "I wish I had taken her for more walks." "I wasn't there at the end." "It's my own stupid fault." "I gave her the chicken bone." "Putting her down was the most awful thing I've ever done." "I wasn't patient enough with him in his old age." "He counted on me and I let him down."

We seem to let go of the guilt, and then cycle back around to it. "Why did I...?" and then "Why didn't I...?"

Guilt can be seen as part of the denial stage, a way of hanging on to those moments before the curtain fell. As long as we can keep replaying our own part in the painful story, we have the fleeting illusion of being able to change the outcome. Had we done something differently, our pet would have had a happier life or would not have died. We had control. That's what we are telling ourselves as we cycle back through Guilt time and again.

When we are mourning a spirit that depended on us in a child-like way, the guilt seems to make sense. Our animal companion depended on us for survival. Our dear friend has died, thus it must be our fault. The very dependence that fosters bonding also fosters a sense of responsibility, and when sickness, accidents or death come, a sense of guilt.

We feel totally responsible for our pets' well-being, and often, we are even called upon to make the very difficult decision to euthanize them when their lives have become a burden to them. That decision is one that leaves many people stricken with guilt and second-guessing. "Did I wait too long? Did I selfishly let him suffer because I couldn't let go?" Or, on the other hand, "Did I move too quickly? Could she have had one more good week? Was she ready to go?"

While the guilt *seems* to make sense, and may even be a necessary stage to pass through on our path to healing, in actual fact the guilt is usually irrational. Most of the time, in our interactions with our animal companions, we are doing the best we know, as the imperfect and limited human beings we are. Not all accidents can be avoided. We cannot expect ourselves to know every precaution to take. We cannot look back and expect ourselves to have been able to predict outcomes. We act from love. We also act from ignorance sometimes. Accepting both aspects as human and forgivable, we can heal.

As we struggle with the guilt, and sometimes let it win and wash over us in a painful wave, we can observe that feeling and let it be. As we sit with a feeling, it tends to change. So when we're ready to allow another feeling, we can try this: How would our animal companion want us to feel right now? What did he or she always want us to feel?

As we consider those questions, we may feel a kindling in our hearts of that joyful love, that very pure connection that our animal gave us—and will always give us, whenever we go to this place of feeling that loving intention, that unique energy shared between human and animal.

In this heart-place, the relationship continues to develop, even after death. The guilt is calling your attention to the pain of separation. As your grief works through you, you will come to feel that your connection with your animal remains within you, and the relationship is always there.

Kevin, George and Gracie: A Loss of Identity

Kevin was a 58-year-old man, his hair turning white. It was the night of an important Blackhawks game, and Kevin was wearing his Blackhawks jersey. He was missing the game to come to the pet grief group, because, he said, "This is more important."

A year earlier, Kevin had suffered the loss of his Schnauzer, George. He had been heartbroken, but at least he still had his other schnauzer, George's close buddy, Gracie. The two had been littermates, and were inseparable throughout their lives. They had passed at 16 and 17 years of age, respectively.

"They saw me through so many things. Relationships, break-ups, job changes, the death of my father. They were there for every significant thing, good or bad. Back when I got them, it was still the nineties! My hair was still brown!" Kevin laughed through his tears.

13

"I'm still talking to them. Is that normal?"

Yes, it is. Many bereaved pet guardians report that they continue to converse with their animals after they have passed on. It gives comfort.

"My dogs always slept in my bed with me. Every morning when I wake up, my first thought is to notice where my dog is. That's when I remember, she's not here anymore. Then my heart sinks, and the pain of it all hits me again, like the first time.... I don't want to get up.... What should I get up for?"

Kevin showed pictures on his phone of George and Gracie at parties, George and Gracie at outdoor restaurants in Chicago, George and Gracie in their neighborhood.

"Everyone knew them. Maybe they didn't know me, but everyone knew my kids. 'My kids'—that's what I called them, and that's how I think of them. Now when I walk outside my apartment, I feel strange: I'm all alone. It's like I'm not the same guy, without them. It's like they were my identity. I don't know who I am without them. Is that crazy?"

Kevin may have had some doubts if he "should" feel so much pain about his dogs, but he had the healthy intention to acknowledge his feelings. He memorialized his dogs by sprinkling their ashes over his father's tombstone. "My father just loved those dogs, and they loved him, too. I hope they are together now."

Kevin said his friends were all supportive of his grief. They had all loved the famous duo as well, and knew how much they meant to Kevin. "I even told some of them that I'm coming here. They were like, 'Wow, man, you really think you need *psychological* support?' and I'm like, 'Hey, it's helping me. That's all I can tell you,' and they say, 'Well, good then. Do what you have to do.'"

Kevin is lucky to have friends who support his mourning process. Pet grief is called a "disenfranchised grief," meaning that it is a grief not recognized by society as a whole. Animals generally do not have the same status as people; pet guardians who deeply grieve the loss of their animal companions are sometimes reminded that, "It was just an animal, you know," and are told, "You can always get another one."

These remarks are made by people who are uneasy seeing another person grieve and want it to stop—for the sake of their own comfort. These remarks are also made by people who have never experienced a truly deep bond with an animal—or who choose not to acknowledge or remember if they ever did.

As a result of these remarks and attitudes, mourners often feel embarrassed by their own grief, and as if they do not have a right to feel the feelings they have, or as if they must be "crazy" to care so much about an animal.

If your relationship with your pet was so strong that he or she became a part of your identity, you may have the feeling that you are not sure who you are when your pet passes away.

Margaret, a resident of suburban Chicago, was known as "Rosie's mom." Her mixed breed rescue dog was a neighborhood favorite, known for her friendly disposition toward everyone. People looked for her as they passed Margaret's house, and would usually see Rosie gazing with calm interest from her living room window. When Margaret planted flowers, raked leaves, or shoveled snow, there Rosie would be, playing or resting by Margaret's side. Margaret walked Rosie for 3 miles every day, and

Rosie grew to know the people they would encounter, and they grew to know and look for her. Margaret and Rosie were seen as a pair.

This type of relationship, where the pet is so much more than a pet, where the human finds in the animal companion a best friend, partner, and sidekick, where the human and the animal companion become known as a duo, is one that is often devastating and confusing to lose. People sometimes say, "It's not just that I've lost an important part of me; I feel like I've lost all of me."

This is not unusual in the experience of grief. Those who are closest to us may seem to be part of our identity: we are someone's partner, parent, son or daughter. Grief turns our world around to the point that it may seem unrecognizable.

Although this confusion and loss may lead to despair, you can be sure that this is normal, and that it is a part of the process of grief. Trust in the process, and allow yourself to feel all the feelings. Find a safe person with whom to talk, someone who will not mind if you repeat your story, someone who is a patient and kind listener. This may be a friend or a therapist or even a pet loss hotline volunteer.

Through talking it out, writing it out, and perhaps even creating a scrap book of memories, you will find yourself moving through this dark tunnel of grief—perhaps at a slow pace, but moving nonetheless.

Betty & Josie: The Anger of Grief Brings Out Other Painful Issues

Betty's mourning was full of rage.

Betty was a Chinese Canadian student, 26 years old, who had come to Chicago from Montreal to study at Northwestern University. Sadly, she had not been able to bring her best friend with her, a poodle mix named Josie. She left Josie with her parents. One day, her mother informed her in a phone conversation that Josie had died four months previously. She had hidden the fact from Betty, she said, because she did not want to upset her while she was studying. Betty, in shock, immediately dropped out of school.

"The important thing about me, as far as my parents are concerned, is my grades. They love the bragging rights. I am not a full human being to them, with emotions and rights of my own. They always put my achievements ahead of my feelings."

Betty's grief for Josie was complicated by the fact that she was not sure her dog had really died. First there was the normal and typical denial that goes with grief. But then, Betty reflected that she had not actually seen Josie's body. In the past, her parents had often lied to her "for her own good" or for their own convenience, resulting in her complete lack of trust in them. Could it be that Josie was still living? And if so, where? But this train of thought led nowhere. There was no logical end to it, and Betty concluded, although still harboring some nagging doubt, that her dearest friend had passed on while Betty was far away. She angrily asked her mother how she could have left her ignorant of her dog's death. At that, her mother wailed that Josie's death had affected *her* terribly, too, and that she had been in bed for a month after Josie died.

Betty could have recognized here that her mother suffered from the same depression that had plagued Betty for years, but she was too angry to care about that.

17

When she most needed comfort and support, her mother seemed to be making herself out to be the victim of the story.

Betty didn't speak to her parents again after the death of her dog. It had been four years of rage-full silence.

Had Josie been sick, or was the death sudden? Was it an illness or an accident? Was it preventable? Had Josie missed Betty? Had Josie died of grief because Betty had left her? Had Betty's parents caused the death in some way? Betty longed for the answers to these questions.

Josie had come into Betty's life when she was a lonely, depressed, stressed-out high school student. In the cold and highly pressured atmosphere of Betty's family home, Josie quickly became her main emotional support. Betty devoted herself to Josie's care, talking to her, holding her on her lap while she studied, and playing with her to distract herself from her academic and family stressors.

Betty was hospitalized for depression three years after Josie's death. Mental health counselors refused to believe that her deep sadness was due to the death of her pet. "Let's get to the real issue," they always seemed to be saying. They implied that grief over a dog is not a deep enough pain to send someone to the hospital with depression; there had to be something else.

Of course, there is always something else, no matter what the presenting issue may be. We are complicated. However, when counselors and psychiatrists refused to take Betty's grief seriously, she felt her emotions being discounted once again, just as her parents had always disregarded her true feelings. Betty started taking an anti-depressant, and went to counseling after release from the hospital, but she learned to not talk about her dog to the therapist, who did not accept that Josie could have been "that important" in Betty's life.

Even four years after hearing the news of Josie's death, Betty could not talk about her without crying and sobbing as if her heart would break.

Betty began volunteering at PAWS Chicago so she could enjoy the company of cats and dogs and feel that she was helping them, too. While there, she learned about the pet grief group and began attending it, and she found that it validated her feelings to meet others who also were grieving the loss of a pet.

Betty remained in Chicago for four years after her rupture from her family. She began working with a therapist who understood the issue of pet grief and was able to support Betty in her grieving for Josie, while at the same time helping Betty to work through her family of origin issues. Betty decided she would return to her hometown of Montreal. She was looking forward to connecting there with supportive and much-loved old friends. She was unsure if she would contact her parents.

Anticipatory Grief

Jennifer, 46 years old, is an accountant, single, with no children. She always thought she would be married and have children by this point in her life, but that path has never opened for her. She has truly not been sad about this, however, and has enjoyed the last seventeen years with her little golden and fluffy Pomeranian, her "ball of light," Marigold.

Jennifer called me for individual therapy to work on anticipatory grief. Jennifer knew a tremendous loss was coming, and she wanted to get support ahead of time and prepare for it.

"Marigold was my gift to myself for my twenty-ninth birthday," said Jennifer at her first appointment in my office. "She has seen me through a succession of partners, a job loss, a job search, job pressures, all kinds of joys and sorrows. She's the reason I transitioned to working from home. She has come with me on every vacation, has come with me to every family gathering. Where she wasn't allowed to go, I really didn't care to go. She has been my best friend, always loving, always supporting. I talk to her every day. Since she has been ill, I have become her nurse, giving her I.V. fluids, dosing her through the night and day. I really can't imagine a life for myself that doesn't include Marigold."

Jennifer came for individual therapy weekly through Marigold's last two months of life, bringing Marigold, wrapped in a hand-knitted blanket, to the sessions. Marigold, diapered in the smallest diaper ever, tottered unsteadily about the office on her brittle, arthritic legs; she was old-lady-thin and disoriented. "She seems to be having little strokes now," Jennifer explained, smiling through her tears.

After Marigold's death by euthanasia, Jennifer came back to counseling only occasionally. "I'm surprised I'm functioning as well as I am," she said. "I know that all that counseling beforehand, and having the time to prepare in advance, must have helped a lot. I grieved so much while she was still here, and I could talk to her and show my love for her. I still cry when I think of her, but it's not unbearable, like I thought it would be. I feel she's still with me, in a way, and yet I've also let her go. It's hard to explain. But I'm almost ready to start looking for another Pomeranian. Or maybe even a small dog of another breed. I'm waiting for Marigold to send me a sign." Jennifer is able to smile, pressing a tissue to her eye, and thinking of her continuing connection to her little golden "ball of light."

If you, like Jennifer with her elderly Pomeranian Marigold, know ahead of time that your cherished animal friend is reaching the end of his or her life, and anticipate that this may be very difficult for you, it would be wise to seek out support ahead of time.

Jennifer talked with family members who also loved Marigold, she researched the option of euthanasia at home through a mobile vet service, and she began coming to therapy with me so she would have professional support as she faced this painful separation. Her experience turned out to be that there was more pain before the death than after. She felt she had done the greater part of the grieving while Marigold was declining, and still with her.

Making the Decision to Euthanize

The decision to euthanize your animal companion may be the hardest decision you ever have to carry out. Generally, it's only for our animals that we have this option and responsibility. At the same time, it's our animals who are the most unconditionally loving and the most dependent upon us for their welfare. The end of life decisions are very tough.

Dr. Nathaniel Cook, DVM, has a mobile senior pet veterinary care and hospice service in the Chicago area, and offers these thoughts:

- *Trust your feelings—people who understand their animal will know when he or she cannot go on.*

- *Understand that it is supposed to be a very hard decision—nothing this important can ever be easy.*
- *Understand that it is supposed to hurt—everything that we truly care about is emotional.*

Dr. Kari Trotsky, DVM, is an Illinois mobile veterinarian who specializes in home euthanasia for pets. Here are some of her reflections on making the decision:

"You make the decision out of love. It is awful to watch your pet in pain. If your pet has a terminal condition and living out his life would cause pain, the loss of dignity by soiling on himself, or confusion as to why he can no longer get up and walk like he once did, peaceful euthanasia is your only option."

Dr. Lisa McIntyre, DVM, of the Welcome Waggin' Mobile Veterinary Service in the Chicago area, adds that well-meaning people may advise "'your pet will let you know it is time, or 'Your pet will have a certain look in its eye.' Most of us who have experienced pet loss don't necessarily believe this to be the case.... This statement, while well-meaning, puts undue pressure on people during an already stressful time. 'What if I miss the signs? He looked miserable yesterday but better today. What if I act too soon or not soon enough?"

Animals instinctively mask any weakness or sickness so that they will not fall prey to predators. It can be difficult for you to tell how ill your animal feels. Compassionate veterinarians suggest that you try as best you can to see your pet's situation from his or her point of view.

Dr. Lisa McIntyre says, "You must ask yourself whether your pet wants to be here today, to experience this day in this way, as much as you may want him to.... He needs to know that you will always put his peace before your own, and that you are able to love him as unselfishly as he has loved you."

The Dead House

People who are mourning the loss of a beloved animal companion often mention the pain of the empty house. They come home to the place where they have become accustomed to receiving a celebratory welcome, and instead enter into a silent, sad place.

"This home that Lucy and I loved so much has now become a terrible, dead house," says Cynthia, who is mourning the loss of her 16-year-old cat. "We used to love our home, she and I. Maybe you'd think it's silly, but I used to show her new curtains when I bought them and ask her if she liked them." Cynthia smiles, and then the tears flow. "Now I feel like I hate my house."

It is sometimes said that the cat is the soul of the house. It is also said that a home is not a home without a dog.

If you have other animal companions, you may not feel this aspect quite so intensely. Having other pets does not lessen your pain on losing one, especially if the attachment was deep. But what I now call "the dead house feeling" can be overwhelming when there is no wagging tail at all, or no sauntering, vocalizing feline to greet you at the door.

When you sit at your computer and look down to where your pet would lie, you remember you are alone. When you go to the kitchen to make a pot of coffee, no one is excited to rise and strut or spin alongside you, hoping for a treat or a snuggle while you pour your brew.

When you wake up in the morning, silence. No fur to touch. No little being imploring you to get up and bust out the kibble.

Kendra says, "I have had to euthanize four English setters over my lifetime. Before this last time, I always had another, younger setter at home. I see now how much that must have eased my pain. This last time, when I had to let Delilah go, it was the first time I left the vet's and didn't have a dog to come home to. Someday— not right away—I'll have another dog. But I think I'll stagger them now—always have another, younger one. This pain of having no animal at all is like nothing I've ever known. It's like...maybe this is nutty...it's like I don't know what to do with myself. Like, what's my purpose?" Kendra laughs softly. "Honestly. I have a family; I work from home and love my work. You would think I had a purpose. But I keep wanting to grab Delilah's leash, and then I remember, she's not here. It's such an empty feeling."

If you are experiencing this "dead house feeling," just know that it is normal. While our animals are with us, we may take their constant company and interest in us for granted. We get used to it and don't realize how supportive it is until it is gone.

Know that when you are ready, there is no shortage of homeless animals who would be grateful to share your life with you. Remember that your animal companion only wanted you to be happy, and it is not disloyal to love another pet. Don't rush it. Mourn fully, and let your grief subside in its own time. And then heal, and love again.

When Others Don't Understand

If you had a close bond with an animal companion, and he or she has passed away, you may find yourself feeling that a part of you is gone.

Sometimes, it's hard to find anyone who understands. The people who are closest to you may say the most foolish things.

They try to put it in perspective when they say, "It was just a pet." They try to be helpful when they say, "Get another one." They don't know that these are the unkindest things they could say, because remarks like these show that they do not understand the depth of your attachment to your friend.

For you, "just a pet" does not describe the relationship you had. Your animal companion may have accompanied you through many stages of life, and was often your best support. Many people say that their pet was truly their best friend, and that they would actually have preferred to spend time with their pet than with most people they could name.

As for "getting another one," when your heart is broken, this is probably not what you want to hear. Someday, when you have healed, you will think about that, perhaps. But people who want to rush you into replacing your irreplaceable friend are not helping.

When they exclaim, "What? You're still upset about that animal? It's been (x amount of time)!" here is something you can tell them: "I have lost a member of my family. I don't expect you to understand, but I do expect you to respect my feelings."

Do not allow anyone to rush you through this grief, any more than you would be rushed through grief following the death of anyone else important in your life. Allow yourself to go through all the stages of reaction to death: denial, anger, bargaining, guilt, yearning, depression, and acceptance.

You have the right to grieve, and you have the need to grieve. You have had an important loss, and need time to work through it, and to let the grief work through you.

Helpful ways to mourn are to have some kind of ceremony to say good-bye and to make a memorial for your pet. You may want to put keepsakes such as tags, collar and favorite toy in a decorative box. (See the section on Memorializing for a more thorough discussion.)

When you are feeling low, remember how your animal companion comforted you. What would he or she want you to feel now? Realize that you have your friend in your heart, internalized, for the rest of your life, and that love remains with you.

The Six Worst Things to Say

If you care about someone who is having a hard time following the death of a cherished animal companion, you probably would like to say something to help the person resolve the grief and begin feeling better.

Please, do not say any of the six most common things that are said to people grieving a pet.

1. "It was just an animal."
   Yes, it *was* an animal, and the person completely understands this. It was an animal that was also an emotional support, a member of the family, and

so much more. You would not say "It was just a ---fill in the blank" for any other loss. "Just a grandmother." "Just a best friend." This is no different. Although you may not think *you* would ever have such a deep relationship with an animal, this does not mean that your friend is wrong to have loved an animal companion so much.

2. "Why don't you just get another one?"
   This is not the loss of a cell phone. This is the loss of a unique relationship. With time, your friend may be ready to invite another animal companion into his or her life. Rushing a new pet in will not help, and may hinder the grieving process. The person has to be ready, and he or she is the best judge of that.

3. "Aren't you over that *yet?*"
   This implies a judgment, and an impatience on your part. No one wants to stay stuck in grief. Coming out of a grieving period takes more than a simple decision to do so. Allow your friend to take the needed time, to mourn, to resolve the grief naturally. If your friend seems to be stuck in grief, you could help by finding the name of a professional counselor who understands pet grief, and passing that name along. This would show that you understand that this process is hard, and is worthy of attention.

4. "Other people have greater losses." Your friend knows this. And it doesn't lessen the pain one bit. Again, it feels like a judgment when you imply that this significant loss is not a big deal in the grand scheme of things. To your friend, it is very painful.

There is no use in comparing one person's pain to another's. It doesn't help.

5. "You shouldn't feel this way." We all have a right to our feelings. Feelings need to be acknowledged and understood. If you find yourself wanting to tell your friend to not feel the feelings, take a look at your own comfort level with your own feelings. Are you also intolerant of your own emotions? To live fully, we must experience all the colors of life, even the sadder ones. We needn't fear our feelings. If we sit with them, they change.

6. "It's time to move on." This is no one's call but the griever's. While it is true that an unresolved grief can become a chronic depression, and that is something to be avoided, it is no one's right to put a time limit on another person's grief. Again, professional help can be suggested. But allow your friend to move through grief at his or her own pace.

As when supporting anyone with any kind of grief, it is not important that you *say* something. Listening is far more important. Try to be a supportive and kind listener. Acknowledge the sadness that your friend feels. Try to resist the temptation to make a suggestion or push your friend in some direction so that he or she will feel better. Your friend will be very grateful if you say, "I know this is a very difficult loss. I am so sorry. If you would like to talk to me about it, I will listen."

Is This Normal?

You may be surprised by the path your grief takes. Grief takes on a life of its own. It comes into your life, seems to take over your thoughts and reactions, and stays as long as it will—like an unwelcome guest.

People in grief are sometimes puzzled or dismayed by their own thoughts and behavior and may even wonder if they are "going crazy."

What follows is some exploration of what people have shared with me in pet grief groups and in individual therapy. (As always, identifying details are changed, to protect privacy.)

"I am crying—*sobbing*—more for the loss of my cat than I ever cried for my mother and father when each of them passed. And I *loved* my mother and father. They meant the world to me. And yet, this loss is somehow more painful. How can that be? I feel ashamed. I should love my parents more than I love my cat."

These words were spoken by Barb, a 65-year-old divorced woman, but almost exactly the same words have been spoken by grieving people of every description.

Yes, it *is* normal to feel this loss more painfully than the losses of some people in your life—even people who were very dear to you. If this happens to you, you will know that this is not as strange as it might seem.

Feeling this loss even more than you felt previous ones does not mean that you loved any of your dear ones more—or less; it does not mean one relationship was deeper and another shallower. There is no need to compare. Grief cannot be compared in that way; judging yourself for the depth of your grief is not necessary, and doesn't help.

Your relationship with your pet was unique. In all likelihood, your pet was able to be with you in ways people never could: sitting near you while you read or worked, following you from kitchen to computer to bed, taking walks with you, greeting you as you came into the house—or even into the room after a short absence. Your pet was there through all the moods and hours of your day, day in and day out.

You were always the center of things in your pet's world. The relationship was uncomplicated and clean of criticism, resentment, rejection, misunderstandings, and grudges—in short, a truly pure relationship that is very particular to the connection between an animal and a human. No human being could possibly give you that same clear and selfless devotion.

It's very likely that you touched your pet more than you touched even the dearest people in your life; physical touch is a very important part of bonding.

While grieving, you may find yourself talking out loud to your animal companion. Frank, a single man in his fifties, kept up a running dialog with his black cat, Felix, for 17 years. As Frank made his morning coffee, powered on his computer to work from home, and planned his day, he shared his thoughts with Felix, who showed a flattering interest, turning his head from one side to the other, meeting Frank's eyes with his own emerald ones, and vocalizing in a variety of feline expressions, as if to demonstrate that he was following Frank's line of thinking, and wanted to share his own reflections on it all.

"I know Felix didn't understand the words...but I can't help thinking then again, that he *did.* Or he understood the vibe, or something. He got me on his own level, in a way I can't describe." Frank's eyes well with tears, which he tries to push back in with his fingers. "Now Felix is gone—I'm still talking to him. 'What do you think about this, Felix?' Am I nuts, or what?"

Frank is not "nuts." He loves his pet deeply and is grieving deeply. Many people continue to talk to their pets after separated by death.

Cathy, a divorced empty-nester, is grieving the death of her golden retriever, Sasha. Cathy finds herself filling Sasha's water bowl daily, even though Sasha has been gone for a month.

"It seems crazy, stupid, but I feel I have to keep clean, fresh water out for her."

"Do you feel better after you fill the water bowl?" I ask.

Cathy considers. "I can't say that I feel any better. But if I don't do it, I feel awful—overwhelmed with anxiety and hopelessness. So filling the water bowl doesn't make me feel less sad. But it relieves that anxiety I would feel if I didn't do it." She sighs. "I know I need to stop."

In fact, as we explore this, Cathy sees that she does not need to stop. Filling the water bowl is an instinctive part of Cathy's own personal mourning process. It is an outward demonstration of the "denial phase" of her grief: providing the water just as if Sasha were still there to lap it up and spill streams of it on the floor. Cathy can continue filling Sasha's water bowl until she no longer feels the need to do it.

Alithea, a college professor with an impressive academic career, speaks softly of her attempts to preserve Tony the Chihuahua's environment just as it was the day the mobile vet came to her home to euthanize him.

"His downstairs bed and his upstairs bed," she smiles through her tears, "—he had two—they are both just where they were. I won't wash them. I can't even think about putting them away. Everyone is telling me to put them out of sight, and maybe I should, but I just can't. A toy he left out on the living room rug is still right there. He used to make little paw tracks in the comforter on my bed every day. Now he's not there to do it anymore." Alithea gasps and sobs. "So I make little tracks with my fingers, right across the bed, so it looks like he was just there. I feel I have to, to make the bed look right, the way it's supposed to be."

Like Cathy, Alithea is processing her grief, practicing her own mourning ritual, by preserving the home environment as it was before the loss. In this, there can be a sense of control where the heart and mind are struggling with the lack of control we experience when a loved one passes away.

These mourning rituals will continue as long as a person needs them, and then fade out.

Jenna, a woman in her thirties, began her path to wellness and fitness for the first time in her life when she adopted Fran, an energetic border collie. "When I saw her at the shelter, I fell in love, and just knew she was my dog. The shelter worker warned me that border collies need lots of exercise, and that someone had already adopted Fran and brought her back because they couldn't give her the exercise she needed, and Fran, in her boredom, had gotten destructive in the house. At the time, the very idea of exercise horrified me. But I had to have Fran."

To meet Fran's need for consistent vigorous exercise, Jenna walked her a minimum of six miles every day, through rain, snow and sleet. As a result, Jenna found herself arriving at a healthy weight and happier state of mind. For nine years, Jenna and Fran could be seen every day, walking briskly through neighborhoods and parks, and often, to give her a sense of work, Fran carried a small stuffed toy—a squirrel—in her mouth. "Squirrel-squirrel" provided one of the many games Jenna invented to keep Fran's mind busy; Fran learned to find Squirrel-squirrel, to "put Squirrel-squirrel to bed," and many other activities on command.

After Fran's death, Jenna continues her routine of walking, and she feels compelled to carry the stuffed squirrel with her, in her hand or in her coat pocket.

"That silly toy fills me with sorrow and comfort at the same time. It's like Fran is with me when I carry Squirrel-squirrel. It's like I can't let go."

Jenna does not need to let go—not all at once, and not on anyone else's time table. Carrying Squirrel-squirrel seems to provide some peace for now, and does no harm.

"Seeing things" and "hearing things" are another common aspect of grief. David, a man in his forties, is grieving the death of his Rottweiler, Sam.

"In the morning, as I wake up, I hear his tags jingling in the hallway. I jump out of bed, feeling kind of excited, thinking, he's come back, somehow. Nothing's there. Maybe it's Sam, his spirit, visiting me. Or maybe I'm losing it."

Ariana, a college student, recently had to euthanize her orange tabby cat, Shelby. "I'll be walking in town, and it's like I see her. It's not a cat that sort of looks like her. It's Shelby herself: exactly Shelby. My heart starts beating so fast. But whenever I can get up close, I can see then, it's not Shelby. In fact, suddenly it looks nothing like her at all. It's freaking me out, seeing her in random places, and then realizing it can't be. It's my mind playing tricks."

Both David and Ariana are experiencing common grief reactions that probably spring from the deep yearning to see or hear the loved one again, and so the mind provides what we so much want to hear and see. This, like all the other grief reactions, will fade away in time.

Other grief reactions include:

- Ruminating (cycling through the same unhappy thoughts again and again)
- Guilt
- Deep mournful sighs
- Flashes of anger: towards your vet, friends, family, God, yourself, and even your animal companion (for getting sick or "leaving")

Knowing that all of this is normal, you will be spared, I hope, from unnecessary self-judgments or worry about your sanity while grieving the loss of your pet. It's always a good idea to find a professional therapist who understands pet grief, just to give you the support you need as you work through your grief.

Replaying the End

When your grief is raw and new, you may find yourself replaying the last scene of your pet's life—or perhaps the days of the last illness-- again and again. This is called "ruminating." Your mind may seem compelled to go back to that time, and you may want to tell that part of the story to kind listeners. You are not being morbid or dwelling on the negative. Your mind is trying to process that this sad thing, which seems surreal, has actually happened. Through thinking it through repeatedly, your mind is trying to move you towards acceptance.

How Long Will I Feel This Way?

As I work with people in deep grief after the loss of a cherished pet, I hear many questions again and again. One of them is: "How long will I feel this way?"

The intensity of the pain is so great that you may be surprised by it, and may wonder how long you can stand to feel such a deep sense of loss. On the one hand, you may be hoping that this emotional suffering is close to ending. On the other hand, you may not want to feel the pain end, because you fear that this would signal you have "moved on," and you are not ready for that yet.

The answer to the question, "How long will I feel this way?" is an unsatisfactory one, because it offers no clarity. Grief takes as long as it takes. It is highly individual.

As mentioned earlier, Kubler-Ross is famous for delineating "stages of grief," but she never meant to imply that these stages follow a linear progression. Rather, they are part of the myriad feelings that grievers experience: Denial, Anger, Bargaining, Depression, and Acceptance. You may find you experience more than one of these at a time, that you loop back and experience some or all repeatedly. You may not experience all of them.

At the end, however, comes Acceptance, which offers some level of peace. There is no way to rush to Acceptance and skip all the feelings and difficult emotional experiences that must come before it. The people in your life who love you and want you to be happy might like to push you along towards Acceptance, but it doesn't work that way.

Grief has a life of its own. Grief takes its own time.

The reason it takes a long time to get to Acceptance is that you have invested your love in a dear fellow-creature who played, no doubt, many roles in your life. This may be an animal friend who was also an emotional support. Perhaps he or she saw you through important milestones in your life. When you give your heart and then lose your loved one, a wound is created that may feel as if it will never heal.

In addition, you may go through a long period of time when you don't really want to heal yet. And that is okay. There is a wise part of you that knows that you need to take your time through this transition to life without your animal companion.

Sometimes there is an emotional block to healing. For example, you might feel that you would be disloyal if you would begin to heal. In time, it will make sense to you when you read or hear: "Think of how your pet would want you to feel, and try to feel that way." But when confronted with that statement before you are ready, you will feel that it doesn't apply to you, or that it is a cruel and insensitive statement.

If your friends, family, and others in your life are pushing you along, expressing surprise ("You're still upset about that?"), know that this usually stems from one of two reasons:

1) They love you and are uncomfortable seeing you sad.

2) They have not allowed themselves to fully grieve their own losses, and seeing you do it makes them aware of their own pain which they would rather push away.

In either case, other people's problem with your grief is not your problem, and has nothing to do with you, really. If they don't want to listen or support you in your sadness, or don't know how to, be sure to find support elsewhere.

Finally, "how long you will feel like this" isn't so much the point, as "what supports can you put in place to help you walk this grief road?"

Part Two: Healing

The Process of Healing

The Process of Healing

Telling Your Story (Again and Again)

"All sorrows can be borne if you put them in a story or tell a story about them."—Isak Dinesen

There is great healing power simply in telling your story to a compassionate listener. That, in part, is the "magic" of psychotherapy and support groups. We, as human beings, need to take our sorrows out of ourselves and put them into a narrative. Our human brains need to try to make sense of our experience, and we do that by communicating the important events of our lives and our feelings about them to other people. Even just journaling—communicating with ourselves—can bring us some sense of peace and resolution over time.

Telling your story once may be all you need. Or you may find that you need to repeat your story several times, to exorcise the power it has over you.

Martina and Lloyd, a couple in their forties, came to the pet grief support group several months in a row after the death of their boxer, Murphy.

Martina is a nurse by profession, and she had been in charge of Murphy's medical treatments at home. In the group, month after month, Martina told the same story: how Murphy first showed symptoms, how the veterinarian made the diagnosis, how Martina followed all the vet's instructions, administered all the treatments, the changing dosages and dietary regimens, Murphy's worsening condition, their reluctance to euthanize, and finally the euthanasia.

She did not talk about her feelings, but reviewed the clinical facts each time.

While Martina felt the need to tell the story again and again, Lloyd sat at her side, looking down, nodding from time to time. He did not share Martina's need to repeat the medical details, but he supported her in her need to do so.

Lloyd told the group, "I'm a man of few words."

Martina rejoined, "Well, Lloyd, what choice do you have, married to me?" and the group smiled with them.

Lloyd cleared his throat. "Like I said, a man of few words. I loved Murphy. Best dog I ever had. Best dog ever," and Lloyd wiped his eyes with the back of his hand, and sighed deeply. He had no more to say. Each time he attended the group, his words were few, but gave him the relief he needed: the healing was in being heard.

While your grief is hurting you, find that compassionate ear, and share the story.

Let the Tears Flow

In our Pet grief groups, as people begin to talk about their raw and painful loss, they very often cry. Almost as often, they will apologize: "I'm sorry. I didn't want to do this. I don't usually cry like this."

Even when alone, sometimes people try to stop their tears, as if by stopping the tears, they could stop the pain.

The reverse is true.

We know now that tears that are cried from emotion have high levels of a hormone called cortisol, which is released when we are under stress. It seems that tears are the body's way of cleaning out these stress-related toxins. Tears seem to relieve our emotional pain in a unique way.

Tears release endorphins as well—just as exercise does—this causes us to feel a bit better, a sort of release.

Tears are also a way of communicating, if only with yourself, the sadness that you feel. Our feelings need and deserve to be experienced and acknowledged.

Go ahead and let yourself grieve, mourn and cry.

Never be afraid of your feelings; they are what make you real.

Memorializing

Grief is what we feel after a loss; mourning is what we do to show our grief. One constructive and healing way to mourn is through memorializing. Here are some examples:

- Journaling: writing entries to or about your pet; writing all the good things and all the happy memories so that you will never forget
- a bench dedicated to your pet's memory to place in your garden
- a tree you can plant in your yard or in a park, dedicated to your pet
- a donation to a cause that you or your pet would like
- a decorative box in which you can place collar, tags, favorite toy, and other items belonging to your pet; this can be placed on a shelf in your living room or bedroom
- a shadow box with memorabilia from your pet
- a scrap book showing all the good times

- sprinkling the ashes in a place that is significant for you and your pet
- jewelry that can be made with your pet's picture, paw print or engraved name
- a paw print made in plaster while your pet is still living or just after the death
- A big party inviting everyone who knew your pet; one woman created a flyer-type invitation and had the party at Chicago's famous Lake Front. It was a happy celebration of her dog's life. She also had prayer cards made up with his picture, name, and bio, and on the reverse side, a copy of the poem, "Rainbow Bridge."

While the act of memorializing gives comfort to many people, for others it may be too painful. You may find that you cannot or do not want to do any of these things in the early days after your loss, but perhaps later on, you will. The whole point of memorializing is to comfort the people who remain behind. Let go of any "shoulds" at this time, and pay attention to what your own heart wants. Certainly the memorializing is not something you need to do for your pet; your animal companion feels your love regardless. Memorializing is what you will do for yourself if and when you find it helpful and healing.

My Heart Will Go On

Even after death, the relationship goes on. This is an idea that brings comfort to many. You have your animal companion in your heart, a part of you, and as you go on through life, and think of your friend, the relationship continues to develop.

Your perspectives change, your appreciation may increase, and the love is always there. It may be helpful to you to write about how your relationship with your pet goes on, even after death. Here is something I wrote about our wonderful family dog, Buddy:

Whenever we get a big snowfall, my husband and I always think of Buddy, our American Eskimo mix, who loved to run out into snow showers and scoop up the soft snow on his nose, and then roll around in it, making snow-dog-angels.

When our kids would go to the sled hill, Buddy would go, too, running up and down the hill, greeting every man, woman and child there joyfully, beside himself with happiness.

When the kids would be shoveling, Buddy would be right there, lying in the snow, soaking in the crystal white ambience.

When the children would make a snowman, there would be Buddy, running in circles, playing, and guarding "his kids."

"There was never a dog like him," I say, whenever we get a good Chicago snowfall.

"There will never be another," my husband says, looking out into the snowy yard that Buddy would have loved to dive into.

"What a great dog," our (now grown) children say, remembering the sled hill.

And although we loved and appreciated Buddy at the time, I think our understanding of his special qualities continues to grow as time goes by.

We remember when we first got him as a pup. We had stopped in at a local shelter "just to look," and came out with what looked like a little polar bear cub. He grew to be a strikingly beautiful dog, with a swagger and a smile that would make you think he understood full well what a charismatic impression he made.

He was gentle and tolerant, and tuned in to the emotions and needs of his human family.

Even now, five years after his death, I feel a warmth in my heart when I think of Buddy. I feel his support, his sense of fun, his unwavering optimism that each day was going to be a great one, and each motion I made might result in something good to eat, or an adventure of some kind. And for Buddy, any time spent with his people was an adventure.

Even now, I think of Buddy as one of the important beings in my life, one of those milestone influences whose message of love and support stays with me always. He gave his full attention to making us happy, and he made us feel as if we were his sole purpose in life. He was with our family during the growing up years of our children, and in my mind he stands for everything that was fun and beautiful and full of heart about those days.

I feel that even now, his message to me is, whatever you think it's all about, think again: it's all about the love.

Thank you, Buddy, for being who you were and are. Love you.

Buddy, our family dog from 1995-2006. Photo by Tom Davy.

Taking Care of Yourself in Your Grief

Grieving is exhausting work. It is important to be kind and patient with yourself. Here are some tips to get you through it:

- If you find that your sleep is disturbed, find extra opportunities to sleep or at least rest.

- Eat at regular intervals even if you are not hungry, and choose healthier options such as fruit and vegetables—rather than the sugary sweets that may appeal to you more now.
- Don't judge your feelings, and don't spend more time than you have to with other people who judge your feelings.
- Find a compassionate listener, whether it is a counselor, pet grief hotline volunteer, or a good friend.

Children and Pet Bereavement

How do you support a child through pet grief?

Take your lead from the child, observing what she needs, as this will vary according to the child's age, the intensity of the bond with the pet, and the circumstances of the death. Realize also, that the child will to a great extent take her cues from the adults.

With small children, you will want to avoid the phrase "put to sleep," as children are quite literal in their understanding and may develop a problem with going to bed if they see that after being "put to sleep," their pet never came back again. Euphemisms that we use as adults: "passed away," "passed on," may not be clear enough for a child who is still unclear on what death means. Say simply that the pet died, and give the reason: "because of a bad illness the vet could not cure," or "because he was hit by a car." Tell the truth, but on a child's level. Keep in mind that if the animal died of an illness, the first thing the child will think is, "Will I die when I get an illness?" So if your child asks about that, or if she seems to be worried, address that concern by explaining in easy terms why this illness was fatal—and why it is not the same as illnesses that your child sometimes gets.

Do not hide your own feelings from the child, but instead talk about your own sadness on a simple level, and briefly. A child's attention span is very short.

Encourage your child to draw or talk about her feelings or about her memories of the pet if she wants to.

Do not rush into getting another pet too soon. Bringing in another pet immediately may give the child the impression that animal lives are easily replaceable. Take the time first to mourn this one, and let the feelings settle a bit. Then, by all means, begin to consider saving another homeless animal. At the right time, another pet coming into the home shows the child that although we always remember our friends who have died, there are new friends waiting to join us in our lives as well.

Your Other Pets and Their Grief

Do your other pets grieve when one of them dies?

Many people observe signs that they do.

Cindy was very attached to her black rabbit, Olive. Cindy had adopted a companion rabbit for Olive, Fern, to keep her company while Cindy attended classes at the university. When Olive died, unexpectedly young, Cindy was left with Fern. Cindy's attachment to Fern was not as great; we bond with different intensity to each pet. In Cindy's mind, Fern's main purpose was to be company for Olive, her favorite.

Cindy mourned Olive very deeply. As she would lie in bed and cry, missing Olive, Fern would creep up to Cindy's head and snuggle against her hair, sighing into her ear.

Cindy realized she was not alone in her grief. Fern was grieving as well.

In the hope that a new companion would soften Fern's grief, Cindy adopted another rabbit to keep Fern company. Hazel and Fern bonded readily, and within a week Cindy observed that Fern was behaving like her old self, not showing any outward signs of sadness or grief.

Watching Fern through her tears, Cindy said to her with some resentment, "Well, Fern, you sure got over that fast."

As much as Cindy wanted Fern to heal and be happy, she also struggled with the feeling that Fern's grief should match her own in duration. It took Cindy longer than Fern to begin feeling better.

If you sense that your remaining pet is grieving, you can help by giving her more attention. Dogs will appreciate more outings. Dogs, cats and rabbits will benefit from more play time with you, more games, grooming, massaging, and some special treats.

While we do know that animals grieve for each other, it seems that their grieving is shorter than ours. For one or two weeks, you may observe grief in your remaining pet. If you see grief continuing beyond that point, consider the likely possibility that your pet is actually picking up on your grief, and is being sad along with you, only because of the connection with you. Our animal companions are very attuned to the nuances of our emotional lives.

Visualization at PAWS & the Cat Suites—Mrrrow!

PAWS Chicago is the pet shelter you would want to stay in if you were a homeless pet. When you come to

Chicago, tour PAWS, and you will see what an animal shelter can be with an appreciation of an animal's perspective and with enough funding.

Sponsored by the Hinsdale Animal Cemetery and accompanied by David Remkus, I began facilitating the monthly Pet grief Support Group at PAWS in June of 2013.

The animals at PAWS are not in cages. They stay in rooms that have glass walls on two sides, so people can see in, and animals can see out. On the feline side, the cats stay far from the dogs' area, enjoying their rooms which are furnished with climbing towers and toys. On the dog side, there may be two or three dogs (depending on size and dog-sociability) in each room, which is furnished with special hammock-type beds so that the dogs don't have to lie on the cement floor. Volunteers come in daily to walk and run the dogs along Chicago's Lake Shore so the dogs will be less stressed and anxious.

Upstairs is an area called The Cat Suites, and that is where we had our Pet Grief Support Group meeting one summer night. In attendance were three people who had come to previous meetings and told their stories. Through their shared grief and love of animals, a healing connection had already formed.

Against one wall in this otherwise ordinary meeting room, was a wall of glass behind which were two rows of "apartments" housing cats: single and in compatible pairs. The cats had nooks to hide in and things to play with. As our meeting began, the cats were sleeping, grooming, and quietly occupying themselves as cats do.

Kevin, a man in his forties, had told us in the previous meeting about the painful loss of his two schnauzers— George, one year ago, and Gracie, two weeks ago.

"I just can't wrap my mind around it: they're not here." Kevin spoke haltingly, trying to prevent the tears that wanted to come. "I just want to know they're all right— somewhere, wherever they are—I just want to know they're all right."

"So," I asked, "you would like to know that George and Gracie are in Heaven, or some good place?"

Kevin nodded. "Is that crazy, or what?"

"Not at all. Maybe others have the same feeling." There was assent all around the table.

"Why don't we try something? If you are willing to try this, we could do a visualization, or a guided imagery exercise, where we first relax our breathing, then relax our bodies, and then go to the mind and see our pet in a spiritual and beautiful state. How would you all feel about that?"

Everyone was eager to begin.

We practiced this Guided Imagery, eyes closed, complete relaxation of the body, then going to the mind, seeing the beautiful Light of Spirit, standing at the Entrance to Heaven and knowing that we can visit with our loved one just outside that great gate, the gate opening to let our dear friend come out to be with us, and enjoying a few minutes here: playing, cuddling, receiving or giving a message, or whatever we would like to experience here.

Just as we arrived at the point where the Gates of Heaven opened, the cats in their "apartments"—who had hitherto been silent—set up a chorus of *Mrrooow, mrrooow,*

50

mrrooowing that made it a little difficult for us to stay in our peaceful guided imagery place—and also made us giggle.

The cats, in their exquisite sensitivity, seemed to perceive in the room a state of mind that resonated with them. They perhaps wanted to be a part of our meditative exercise. Although they disrupted our practice in a mild way, they also, at the most poignant moment, reminded us of life, of the animals who are still here and need us, in the here and now.

We came back to awareness of ourselves sitting in that room at that moment and opened our eyes, and the people began to share their experiences. Each person present found the guided imagery very comforting, and so here it is, for you.

You will find it easier to do if you have someone read it to you, or if you use a recording of your own voice reading it.

A Guided Imagery Exercise

(To be read slowly and gently)

Begin by placing both feet flat on the floor, and sitting back comfortably. Let the chair (or couch) support your weight, and close your eyes.

Take a deep cleansing breath.... And let it go. Breathe in slowly and deeply and slowly release your breath, just noticing your breath. Continue breathing. Notice how the air is cool as it comes into your nostrils, and warmer as it goes out.... Breathe in, maybe to the count of four in your mind ...and breathe out to the count of five.... As you continue to breathe slowly, know that you are slowing your pulse rate, slowing your heart rate, and bringing your mind to a state of alert relaxation—all with your own slow, deep breaths.

Continue to breathe evenly now, as we relax the body, starting with the crown of your head. Imagine your scalp relaxing at the top of your head. Smooth your brow. Relax the area around your eyes...your cheek bones...your mouth...your jaws.

Take a deep breath...and let it go...and relax your neck. You could even turn your head from side to side if you like, to notice the relaxation as it spreads down your neck. Take a deep breath, and let it go.

Relax your shoulders. You could imagine your shoulder blades sliding right down your back. Take a breath and release it.

Relax your upper arms...your elbows...your forearms...wrists...hands...and fingers, all the way down to your fingertips, and any tension that is in your body can go flowing out through your fingertips, leaving your arms feeling totally warm, heavy and relaxed.

Continue breathing, in and out. Relax your chest.... Acknowledge your happy, healthy, beating heart with gratitude.... Relax your gut...your stomach...your waist...your hips. Relax your glutes.

Continue breathing. Relax your thighs...your knees...your calves and ankles. Relax your feet...and toes. And any stress that was still in your body can go flowing out now through your toes, leaving your legs and your entire body warm, peaceful and relaxed.

Now take a mental scan of your entire body, as you continue your breathing, and just notice where you've tensed up again—because we usually do; that's okay—and just send warmth and relaxation to any part or parts of you that need more relaxation.

And now that the body is *totally relaxed*, let's go to the mind, where you see yourself standing in a beautiful spiritual light. This is the light that you brought with you when you came into the world. It is a healing and protecting light that has been with you all the time, a light you can always go to. We always know it's there, but sometimes we just forget about it.

So, continuing to breathe, notice your beautiful light. Notice if it has a color today, a temperature, and anything else that you see or feel about your light. Whatever you see is all right: this is your own light, healing you in mind and body, protecting you on every level, and giving you peaceful energy.

Continue your peaceful and even breathing. As you enjoy your light, notice that you are standing by the Entrance to Heaven, the Rainbow Bridge, or to the perfect place your loved one has gone. This Entrance can look any way you see it: pearly gates or a wooden door or hanging beads...or anything you choose.

The most important thing is: your pet is on the other side, and you have come for a visit. Your pet will be allowed to come out and visit with you, not only now, but also any time you choose to practice this guided imagery. So now, see your pet appearing and coming to you....

I will be silent for a few moments while you spend these few moments with your animal companion, any way you would like to: playing, cuddling, talking, and just being together again.

(Allow seven deep breaths of silence to allow the person time here.)

Take a deep, cleansing breath and let it go. Know that after your visit, your pet is going back. However, in the spirit world, a soul can perhaps be in two places at the same time. So your pet, while on the other side, can also be in your heart in a very *real* way.

So if you like, you can take your pet and put him or her in your heart. See that happening, and notice how it feels now, to have your pet staying in your heart in this special way.

Now, even though your pet is going back through the Entrance to Heaven, or the other side, you are also standing with your pet as a part of you, to carry with you always.

Take another deep breath, and release it.

Now, taking our time, we will slowly prepare to come back to this place and this time.

Wiggle your fingers and your toes, take a few more cleansing breaths...flutter your eye lids. As you return to the here and now, you find yourself feeling alert and refreshed.

Take your time, and only when you are ready, open your eyes.

The Visitation Dream and Other Signs

Many people have reported dreaming vividly of their deceased pet. It is usually a happy dream of holding and playing with their animal friend again. Sometimes the dreamer seems to receive a message from the animal companion, such as, "I am happy now; don't worry about me."

Grace, who comes to the pet grief support group to tell the story of her dachshund Buttons, says, "My husband has had *two* of those dreams already. I want Buttons to come to *me* in a dream. Every night, I ask her to come to me in a dream, but she never has. I wish I could see her again, even if it's just in a dream."

Lana says that although she hasn't had a dream, she does at times feel "a comforting presence." Lana says, "In my mind's eye, I see the park I used to walk her to, I see the vacations we took together, and I feel she's telling me, 'You did a lot for me. We had a wonderful life together. Thank you, and be happy now.'"

Some people see signs that they feel their loved one is sending them, indicating love, peace, or well-being. A song comes on the radio, and Joel remembers singing that song to his Rottweiler Harvey, and feels the connection all over again. Christine's thoughts on a bleak and cold day turn to her Bengal cat Javaka, and suddenly the sun bursts through the clouds; she feels that this bright warmth is sent to her from her loving friend on the other side. Francie notices the large black bird that perches on the railing of her deck and cocks his head at her, not startling or flying away when she looks up to meet his gaze. "My dog Lorenzo was solid black with that blue sheen, like a crow. I look at this crow, and the crow looks at me, and I say, 'Is that you, Lorenzo?' and then I laugh at myself and hope nobody heard me. But really, who's to say?"

Just as grief seems to have a life of its own as it works through us, so does healing. Sometimes the form that healing takes is in these dreams, sensations and

55

thoughts. They may be our way of comforting ourselves, or perhaps they really are communications from beyond. As Francie says, "Who's to say?"

Spirituality and Pet Loss: a Search for Meaning. Signs. Rainbow Bridge.

How does your grief affect your spirituality?

And how does your spirituality affect your grief?

Barb, after the passing of her black cat, Mona, found that she became very angry when she attended church. "God took her away from me. She was a young cat, with all her life ahead of her. God punished me—for what, I don't know—I must have done something terrible for such a punishment. I felt I needed to show God my anger by not going to church for a long time."

Jennifer, on the other hand, found herself seeking her connection with the Divine even more after her Pomeranian, Marigold, died. "I pray that she is in some beautiful place. I pray that Spirit will send me another beautiful dog-spirit to care for, when the time is right. I trust that Marigold was sent to me, and that everything now is as it is supposed to be, even though I miss her so much."

Clergy is divided about whether animals have souls, and whether animals are admitted to Heaven. A good book for you to consult if you would like to explore this topic is *The Souls of Animals* by the Reverend Gary Kowalski, a Unitarian Universalist minister.

In the words of Linda Harper, the psychologist who heads the pet grief support group for the Chicago Veterinary Association, "Animals are so pure in heart, so loving and giving, so good! If *we* think *we human beings* can get into

Heaven, how much more likely is it that animals will be there, because they are so much better than we are!"

Some people hold the belief that their pets reincarnate. My father always said he thought our orange tabby cat Ginger was the reincarnation of his red-haired mother. He had a childhood memory of bringing home a stray orange tabby kitten in the 1920's. His mother would not allow him to keep the kitten, although he pleaded, he hoped flatteringly, "But Mother, she has the same color hair as you!" This bit of charm did not soften my grandmother's heart one particle, and out the kitten went, to fend for itself. In the 1960's, when we had a cat with a similar appearance, my father speculated that perhaps it was his mother's karma to come back and live with him as an orange tabby cat. Ginger, by the way, was well-loved by my father, and lived a long life with our family.

How Has Your Pet Changed You?

As part of your healing, you may find it helpful to reflect on how your pet has changed you.

Kevin became known in the neighborhood because of his schnauzers George and Gracie. "I never was the type of person to talk to passersby or to neighbors," said Kevin. "But George and Gracie grabbed attention wherever we went. I learned to be more open and friendly. As a result, I even developed relationships with a few neighbors who always had a treat or a kind word for my dogs."

Rhonda, attending a pet grief group meeting, said that Peanut, her Chihuahua, had made her more affectionate and expressive. "People who know me would describe me as cold. I can't help it; it's just how I am. But somehow, with Peanut, I was totally different. He needed love and protection from me, and my family couldn't believe how I could show him affection and look after him so carefully. He brought out something in me that I didn't even know was there."

Betty, the Canadian student, said that Josie kept her in touch with the fact that she is more than her academic record. "My parents and my teachers saw me as just a high-achieving student, as if only that one dimension mattered. I could have believed that version of myself, too. But Josie didn't care anything about my grades. She made me see who I really am, inside."

How has your animal companion changed you?

You might want to journal about this, to pull out ideas that are lying just below the conscious level. You could also draw a picture to express this in symbolic form.

How Has Grief Changed You?

While grieving, you will go through various changes. After some time, as the grief settles, you may find that your grief experience has changed you in some lasting way.

Barb said, "I think about my friends differently now. I know that not everyone understands pet grief, or how I could bond so much with my cats. But it seems to me that now as I look at my friends' support or lack of support, a line divides them. My oldest friend, June, has always been very cold, and I know that about her, but I have always accepted it. It's just the way she is, and that was always fine. She's not a pet person. We have been friends for decades. But after Mona passed away, June called to invite me to go out to lunch with her, and I mentioned that I was still struggling after the loss of Mona. June said—so coolly—'Oh, is *that* still bothering you? Well, if you're depressed, let's not do lunch now.

Give me a call whenever you feel better.' And that was it! Suddenly, I realized that she doesn't care a bit about my feelings, and that she is no friend at all—despite the decades.

"On the other hand, Lorraine, who is not a pet person either, sent me a plant and a card, and she encourages me to talk to her about how I feel. I'm so grateful to her. It's not that I'm exactly angry with June; I just see her for who she is, and I realize that I don't like who she is. And the friends who have been kind about my loss have much more value to me. I see people in a new light now."

Joe took the loss of his German shepherd, Rufus, very hard. "I've always had shepherds, and each one was such an individual: no two alike—just as individual as people. Rufus was so smart and sweet. He understood every word I said to him, I swear he did. And he understood what I didn't say; he picked up on my feelings and thoughts. After he died I started thinking about that: what a full, complete being he was.

"Then I thought about my mother's cats—each one an individual, with likes and dislikes, ways of communicating, just like Rufus. And I have a buddy who has a parrot that grooms him and shows all her own emotions, and the two of them have a bond just like Rufus and I had.

"That got me to thinking about other animals. Like, what about the raccoons, the squirrels and the deer? What about the coyotes and the foxes? Are they individuals? Do they have relationships and bonds? Just because I don't live with them and see it, doesn't mean they aren't complete individuals, too. And then, what about the cows and pigs? What about chickens? The animals I eat?

"So I started looking into it, and I found out that lambs and pigs will learn to come to you when you call their names; and I read that cows moan and grieve when their calves are taken away from them. And that chickens like to solve puzzles that are created just for them. I got to a place where I thought, all these animals have feelings, just like our dogs and cats do. The only difference is *we* don't feel the same way about *them*. Because we don't know them. After I started thinking this way, I realized that I can't eat meat any more. It's no longer an option for me."

As you begin to gain distance from the death of your pet, you may also notice how grief has left some lasting change in your views on life. Journal about this topic, or express it in some other way, to allow for more growth.

Should You Get Another One?

When your pet passes away, it's very likely that people will ask you, "When are you going to get another one?" If your grief is apparent to them and makes them uncomfortable, they will probably even urge you: "Why don't you *just get another one?*"

You may also wonder, "Should I? Will I feel better if I adopt another animal companion?"

The decision about when to bring another pet into your life is a very individual one. It is most important to not act from what anyone else tells you is best for you. Grief is an inner journey, and while those close to you may accompany you, they cannot effectively direct you, even when you feel lost.

I have observed that when another pet is brought in very quickly, the person tends to compare the new pet unfavorably to the one who has passed away, and sometimes even feels some resentment toward the new one. Eventually, the comparisons will fade away, it is to be hoped, and the new pet will be appreciated for himself or herself.

When the bond was deep, the mourning will be deep as well, and will take some time. One wise person observed, "People say, wait to get a new dog until you stop grieving the old one; but you never completely stop grieving the old one."

At some point, a point that only you will be able to determine, it will be beneficial to you to open your home to a new animal friend. Will the bond be the same? Definitely not. Will the bond be as deep? Possibly. So many things go into creating that deep bond, including shared experiences that are not repeatable. However, there will be new experiences to share, with a new and unique individual.

The bond you had with the old pet is one-of-a-kind, and the same is true of the bond you will create with the new pet. This is why each bond is so precious.

How will you know it is the right time?

This is a good time to let your intuition, your heart, lead you. When the thought of bringing in a new pet fills you with anxiety, resistance or doubt, it is too soon. When the idea feels warm, hopeful and positive, it is time to check out a local adoption event, or do an on-line search, and let the thought begin to grow roots. There is no need to rush; listen to your heart.

Will you feel disloyal to the pet who has passed away? Think of what your pet always wanted for you in life: to see you happy. Some people even ask the spirit of their deceased pet to guide them to the next animal to share their home.

So, should you "get another one"? Yes, you probably should. The bigger question is: "When?" The answer to that lies in your own grief process, and in the willingness to let that unfold with patience.

Fostering at First

Martina and Lloyd, as the months passed after their boxer Murphy's death, began to long for another dog to share their lives and their home. One thing prevented them from moving forward on adopting another dog: Murphy's illness had been long and expensive. Their vet bills were enormous, and it would take a year or more to pay them off. They did not feel they could responsibly adopt another pet until they paid Murphy's bills.

Also, they were unsure if they were truly emotionally ready to bond to another pet.

They decided to try fostering for a local rescue organization. The rescue would pay all the animal's expenses, and Martina and Lloyd would provide shelter, training and socialization. The policy of the rescue they chose was that foster parents are not allowed to adopt the first two animals they foster.

The fostering arrangement would help Martina and Lloyd to keep the emotional distance they wanted at this time, knowing that they were preparing their foster dog for a home with someone else. Martina and Lloyd would benefit by once again having that canine company, that sense of being needed, and the good times that sharing their home with a dog would bring them. They were also made aware, however, that most rescue animals come with one or more issues, and they would need to have patience and tolerance to deal with whatever might come. They were to a point, several months after the loss of Murphy, to deal with this challenge, and to make a difference for another dog.

How Animals Heal Us, and We, Them

What is this mysterious power that animals have to read us, physically, emotionally, and spiritually?

Callie is a black, miniature-sized poodle mix with whom I share my practice. Since the retirement of her predecessor, Dr. Jules (a blind and elderly toy poodle), Callie is my co-therapist. I never tire of watching how she interacts with each of "our" clients in unique ways.

With Charlene, who is grieving the loss of her own poodle and working through a difficult marriage, Callie is very demonstrative: leaning into Charlene, trying to kiss the tears from her face, making Charlene laugh—the only time she laughs all week, she tells me.

When Sam (who is not interested in dogs) comes in, however, Callie does a happy dance around his feet and simply curls up in a circle a couple of feet from him on the couch, where she immediately falls asleep.

One day a young woman called Bridget came in and Callie wagged her tail and went under the couch and did not come back out until Bridget had left. I had never seen Callie do that before. It is the only time she has ever hidden from a client. Bridget was well-groomed, attractive, smiling, interacting with me in a very positive way, and didn't seem to have too much to work on in her session that day. However, later, Bridget told me that before and during our session, she had been secretly seething with anger about her life situation, and was following her usual pattern of not letting her emotions show. The more upset she is, the more "calm, cool and collected" Bridget has learned to appear, due to her years of needing to hide her emotions in her family of origin. She fooled me. She didn't fool Callie.

What is this power of perception that Callie has? She never went to graduate school, never even read an article on body language. Yet she can read a person's inner state—even when that person is concentrating on hiding it—better than I can. It looks as if she is catching some psychic wave, as if she is on a level of awareness beyond the reach of mere human beings.

We've all read and heard true stories of animals sensing tumors and impending seizures, and of animals saving people's lives through this extraordinary and little-understood sense that animals possess.

Doris says that her cat, Catrick, saved her life. One afternoon Doris had a strangely splitting headache and just didn't feel well at all. She had an intuition that she should go to the emergency room, but she didn't feel well enough to drive. She decided to lie down, and hoped she would feel better after a little rest. That's when Catrick, very uncharacteristically, jumped up on her chest and began batting at her hair and face. She rolled over and put him to the side, but he kept coming back to tap at her head and wouldn't stop. Because of his harassment, Doris could not fall asleep, and decided to get herself to the emergency room. There, she was told that she had come in only just in time; she was about to have an aneurism. If she had fallen asleep, she would not have awakened.

Doris adds another dimension to this discussion of how animals heal us. Catrick has also helped Doris to heal from her childhood. Doris was always mocked and bullied by her older siblings and classmates for being overweight. This had caused her to turn inward, and to devalue herself, and to become very sad. As an adult, she found that Catrick and her other cats returned her love in a way that people had not. Her cats were consistently loving, never judging, and she drew an emotional support from them that people had never offered her. She had a sense of safety with her cats, especially with Catrick, that she did not have with people.

This brings us to the cliché phrase that people always use when talking about what our pets give us. I did not want to use that phrase in this book, because clichés are so tiresome that they lose all meaning. And yet, there is a reason a phrase is repeated again and again. Some clichés are simply true: our animals *do* give us *unconditional love.*

Our animals heal us, and we heal them. They need us, not only for food and shelter; they need and want to connect with us on an emotional level. A behaviorist would say that animals only seek our attention because they hope they will be rewarded with food. Yet those of us who have known that close connection with an animal companion know that the relationship is not simply opportunistic. Often, the family pet will bond with a person who is not the one who dispenses the food; for example, sometimes the dog is most devoted to the baby in the house.

Callie, my canine co-therapist, gravitates to people who are sad or anxious. I have the treats at my disposal, and she knows that I give her treats and that clients do not. I have never given her a treat for interacting with a client. Yet when in my office, she always sits with my clients, and never with me. She behaves a little differently with each one, depending on what they are feeling and what

65

she senses they need or want from her. She has nothing to gain, as far as I can see. She is simply a natural healer, fulfilling her life's purpose. I think most animal companions are such natural healers, each in his or her own way.

Health Benefits of Sharing Life with a Pet

The facts on the benefits of having a pet are celebrated in articles you can find in the popular press. Having a pet is good for you, as we all know. We continue to learn more about just how deep the benefits go.

Petting your dog, cat, bird, rabbit, ferret or horse lowers your blood pressure and cholesterol. So there is an immediate, healthful physical response just from touching your pet. Oxytocin, "the cuddling hormone," is released in your brain when you pet your animal for at least three minutes. Your pet experiences this release of oxytocin also. This is the powerful bonding hormone that benefits nursing mothers, giving them a sense of connection to their babies as well as an overall sense of well-being. This peaceful and fulfilled feeling is so rewarding to your brain that you will probably find that you crave it, and seek out your pet just as a nursing mother seeks out her baby. Nature designed this hormone, it seems, to ensure a powerful connection.

People who have pets live longer than those who don't. It seems that people who have a pet are less likely to have a heart attack. Hospital heart patients who have a pet waiting at home for them are more likely to survive and tend to go home sooner.

Why should this be?

Animals make us feel better, and this reduces our stress. As we know, stress is bad for our health.

Playing with a pet can raise levels of serotonin and dopamine, helping people to relax and de-stress, and just feel happier. Pets inspire us to move, laugh, interact and play; these boost the immune system and give us more energy. Some people say that just thinking of their pet makes them feel calmer and happier.

Loneliness has become a common malaise in modern life, and takes a toll on physical and mental health. A pet can provide great relief from loneliness: someone to do "the happy dance" when you come home, someone who is interested in you and longs for nothing more than to spend time with you.

Dogs who need to be walked give us a reason beyond ourselves to exercise. All animal companions that we care for deeply provide us with someone other than ourselves to think about and to live for.

Many people find more emotional support in their pets than they do in human relationships—and this is to say nothing against those human relationships. It's just that a human cannot possibly offer the type of constant support, caring and around-the-clock availability that an animal can.

Here are three cases in point:

Danny and Snickers

A teenage client of mine, Danny, experienced a great deal of healing through his horse, Snickers, which his very wise father had bought for him when Danny was seven years old. Danny had suffered an accident in which he was severely burned on his arms and face. All throughout his childhood, he underwent several surgeries, and his appearance made relationships with other children difficult and painful.

Danny was a suburban kid, but his dad found an equine stable close to their home, and started him in riding lessons. Danny immediately took to the horses with an enthusiasm that surprised his dad. At the barn, Danny was a different child: happy and confident. While in school, Danny had difficulty speaking up and seemed withdrawn, but at the barn, he moved with purpose, carried out his responsibilities expertly, and radiated self-esteem.

"Snickers is so happy when I come to the barn. She always understands how I feel—and I always understand how she feels. I have my moods, and she has hers, too. When we spend time together, we both always feel better."

Danny devoted himself to Snickers' comfort and well-being. Instead of being "stuck in his own head," focused on his burn-related issues or on how people viewed him, he was able to move beyond himself and concentrate on Snickers' perspective and needs, and on maintaining their healing bond. As well- intentioned and caring as the people in Danny's life were, they could not do for him what Snickers did.

Karla and Lovey

Karla was a fifth-grader when her parents brought her to see me in my private counseling practice. She was a Mexican-American girl, demure, polite and quiet. Her parents' concern was Karla's lack of interest in anything—even the things she used to enjoy, such as family parties and playing with friends. An intelligent child who had always done well in school, her grades had sunk. She was sorry to be causing her parents concern, and would at times rally and make an effort, but these were short-lived. She had always been a typically active child, but now she only watched TV or napped. Her parents knew that something was wrong and took her to their family physician, who assured them that Karla was physically healthy. Her parents had tried to open conversations with Karla about her apparent loss of interest in everything, without making her feel judged or wrong, but Karla herself seemed at a loss to understand or explain her new apathy towards life.

As a counselor, I had, of course, many hypotheses running through my mind concerning what could be at the bottom of Karla's symptoms of childhood depression: had there been a trauma, or a death in the family? Sexual abuse? Bullying at school or at home? A secret worry or issue? Unanswered questions about puberty or sexuality? Was there a family history of depression?

As I worked with Karla individually and also together with her family, the only hypothesis that seemed to connect was that of a family history of depression. Considering how this depression was affecting Karla's social development, grades, and self-esteem, medication was a possibility that her parents might consider down the road, but first we would use play therapy and talk therapy to see if we could avoid the medication route.

I saw Karla weekly, and our rapport grew as we worked together. She made an immediate connection with Jules, my blind, toy poodle therapy dog, who greeted her with love and kisses and snuggled on her lap throughout our visits.

Inspired by Jules, Karla began campaigning with her parents to get a dog. This was the one and only issue that Karla showed any interest in; and yet her parents hesitated, not being "pet people," and never having had a dog in the house before.

The matter was just about taken out of their hands when a neighbor's dog had puppies—long-haired, golden brown cross-breeds—that they were "giving away to good homes."

When Karla's mother saw her daughter "light up" for the first time in months, playing with the neighbor's puppies, she knew her decision had been made for her. Karla chose a shiny-eyed, affectionate little female pup she promptly named "Lovey."

Lovey bonded to Karla immediately, seeming somehow to understand whose dog she was. Karla astonished her parents by keeping her promise to take complete and full responsibility for Lovey: daily walks, clean water, feeding, and regular bathing and brushing.

In therapy, Karla talked about Lovey with a bright energy that had been lacking in her before. Sometimes, she told me with the frankness of a ten-year-old, she did not want to come to see me because she did not want to leave Lovey at home.

Karla began to take more of an interest in family gatherings and in having friends over, and used these occasions as an opportunity to show and tell about Lovey, and to "socialize" her, as the dog books she read told her she should do. Karla's grades improved, as she did her homework with Lovey on her lap.

Our counseling sessions slowed down from once a week to twice a month and then once a month. When it was time to terminate therapy, I asked Karla if she could compare for me how she was at the beginning of counseling to how she was now, at the end.

"I used to want to be alone and sleep. Now I look forward to things, especially with Lovey."

I asked her to help me understand what had helped her to get so much better, so quickly.

She might have said it was the sand tray therapy, the safe place to talk with an objective and caring adult, or the age-appropriate cognitive behavioral exercises we had done. But, of course, she mentioned none of these.

"Jules is great," she said. "I didn't want to come here in the first place, but when I met Jules, I liked him, and I only came back to see him." (My counselor's ego does take a beating sometimes when clients give my therapy dog all the credit.)

"But I know the real reason I'm happy now is because I have my own dog." With the simplicity of a child, Karla said, "Lovey makes me happy."

There is a special synergy that happens between people and animals. We are understanding more of the science behind it all the time, but some of it may not be analyzable or describable in words. Lovey gave Karla the opportunity to be responsible, and to have something to show and tell about; Lovey made Karla feel completely accepted and wonderful for being herself with no judgments in a way that mere human beings simply cannot do; Lovey provided Karla with touch, affection, play, a listening ear, and an identity as Lovey's person. And yet, Lovey's way of healing Karla is ultimately, perhaps, beyond words.

Karla herself said it best, in a way that is true and truly beautiful: "Lovey makes me happy." Our animals make us happy. Simple as that.

Even in Darkness, a Rose Can Bloom

Jackson was a 16-year-old client: a young man who had gotten into some trouble and subsequently graduated from military school. He had social anxiety, a disorder which causes a person extreme discomfort in social situations, to the point of blushing, becoming speechless, or just avoiding people altogether. The root of this issue, in my experience, is shame: the feeling that one is somehow bad, wrong or defective, and a feeling of terror that others will see one's defect. Jackson's social fear kept him at home for the most part, with only a few exceptions. Because of the social anxiety, he had not been able to keep a job. He came to me from a hospital Day Program, and was worried that his disorder would limit his life so much, that he wouldn't have a future. This concern was leading him into depression.

When he came in for his first appointment and met Dr. Jules, my blind, white toy poodle therapy dog, he lit up. Because of his social anxiety, it had been very hard for him to come into the office, but he forgot himself when Jules greeted him with such jubilation. Jackson confided that although he loved all animals, he really liked *big* dogs, and wished he could have a big dog himself. His father was against it, and his wish didn't look too promising.

Jackson, Jules and I worked together on the social anxiety issue: understanding how it started and the thought distortions that drove it, and techniques he could practice to begin to move beyond it. Jules greeted Jackson happily each time he came in, and sat supportively by his side as Jackson did his work in therapy.

Jackson, highly motivated to change his life, was making progress: two steps forward and one step back. One day, he and his mother came in and told me that Jackson had gotten a puppy: half Mastiff and half Great Dane. I celebrated with them, and added, "You do realize you will have a pony in the house?" Jackson's mom smiled and nodded and Jackson laughed. He said that this dog would be a therapy dog, like Jules. He already has her registered for the first level of classes she will need.

"What did you name her?" I asked.

"I gave her a special name, since she's going to be a therapy dog. There's a quote I like: 'A rose can bloom, even in the darkness.' So I named her 'Rose.'"

Rose knows she is Jackson's dog, and wherever in the house he goes, she is at his side. When he leaves the house, she sleeps in her corner of the basement and waits for him.

Jackson told me that a big dog like Rose needs a lot of exercise, so this teenager-- who could not take a walk beyond his own block--takes her for long daily walks and runs to the park, and keeps her walking and running so she can get tired out.

Jackson's mother said she doesn't mind buying a big bag of food once in a while, but Jackson—who when he started counseling was terrified of the very thought of a job interview and of working in the public-- will have to get and keep a job so he can buy the food and pay for the vet visits.

Jackson grinned, radiant with joy and purpose. I had never seen him so happy, and so confident.

"I'm ready to get a job. I have to do it, to support Rose."

Danny, Karla and Jackson all have in common that they were young people in need of healing for one reason or another, and they are healing through their bond with a special animal friend.

The Animal Rescue Movement: Why Do People Do It?

As we consider the mutual healing between humans and animals, this might be a good place to pause and look at that most interesting of creatures: the Animal Rescuer.

Animal Rescue has grown, as a movement, over recent years. There have always been people in the community who saved animals, long before it was the "cool thing to do." I recall that in a small town I lived in as a child, there was an elderly man, Mr. Kime, who would take in all dogs or cats in distress, treat their illnesses, and find them new homes. Some of these animals, he had to keep, because no one wanted them. He also tried his hand at rehabilitating any injured wildlife that came his way. No one paid him. He was simply known as a caring person who loved all animals and would help you if you found a litter of kittens under your porch, or any wandering stray. The only other alternative back then, in the 1970's, was the pound.

Now, with the help of the internet, Animal Rescuers connect with each other and cooperate to save all the dogs and cats (and other domestic animals) that they can. They are volunteers, trying to get grant money and donations but very often spending their own money, and certainly their own time and energy. They are passionate about saving animals' lives and finding them good homes.

I asked Jackie Wolfe, a psychotherapist, dog trainer, and President of National Yorkie Rescue, *why* people make these sacrifices for animals they will ultimately re-home.

"Everyone comes to it from a different perspective.

"Some of my very earliest bonds were with animals. As I've pieced things together, I realize that my mother had postpartum depression when I was a baby. In those days, a nurse came to do home visits for all newborns. When the nurse came, she saw that I was losing weight. I had to be re-hospitalized. So I think my mom struggled. My dad was the great animal lover, a wonderful father, but he travelled. He brought home a cocker spaniel puppy when I was a baby, and later I would hear how I would chew on the puppy and he would chew on me. We bonded. That was my sibling.

"Emotionally I relate well to animals. Animals gravitate to me.

"I believe that for many rescuers, there was a unique early emotional attachment with animals when other figures were not available.

"For rescuers, the hard part is saying good-bye. Obviously, there've been some I couldn't say good-bye to, because they still live with me!

"Animals change your life. My husband says these animals we have rescued have changed his life—in a very positive way."

Dr. Linda Harper, Ph.D., in her book, *The Power of Joy in Giving to Animals,* describes the animal rescuer this way: "Your soul, your deepest self, is easily touched by any involvement you might have with animals.... You have a natural desire to give to the animals and a unique ability to receive the gifts that they offer in return."

Jean Lazarro, President of Cry for Help Rescue based in Woodridge, Illinois, when asked why she makes the efforts and sacrifices she does for animals, says, "They deserve it! Animals don't ask for a lot. They don't think you owe them anything. You just give them food and a place to stay, and they're happy."

I asked Jean if she bonded with animals at an early age. "I wasn't exposed to animals as a kid. I had a really bad childhood. I slept in lots of hallways in the city of Chicago, my alcoholic father was abusive to us, and I was locked up in institutions. Maybe that's part of it: seeing animals locked up, seeing them coming from abusive situations. When I see the fear in an animal's eyes, it reminds me of the fear I felt as a child. I can do something about it now. There are so many horrible things happening to animals, and somehow I want to protect them. And...you can't give up. If you give up, you're just one more person not helping. You know you can make a difference, if you just don't ever give up."

Jean loves the goodness in animals. "Animals are straight up. What you see is what you get."

I remarked that people are so much more complicated, so much more a mix of good and bad, than animals are. I asked Jean if her experiences in life have shown her that animals can be trusted not to hurt us; people, on the other hand, are more difficult to predict. She agreed that there might be something in that.

Jean says that a woman in the grocery store, on inquiring about the massive amounts of pet food in Jean's cart, observed, "You should be fostering children instead of animals."

Jean answered kindly, "I believe we should all do what we feel we're called to do, to make the world better. If fostering children is your passion, you should do it."

"Oh no," said the woman, "*I'm* not going to foster any children."

Jean laughs. "People are funny."

Ultimately, it's not a choice between helping animals or people. By saving the animals, rescuers are also helping the people who will one day welcome the animals into their homes, and those people will find their own healing and happiness through these animals. And as Jean says, if we all do our own part in our own way to make the world a better place, everyone wins.

I feel that those who rescue and those who adopt rescued animals, whether always consciously aware of it or not, are healing themselves of past hurts, and are showing themselves that they can do one small thing at a time to overcome some of the suffering in this world.

Equine Assisted Therapy: Horses Healing Humans

Linda De Francisco, Ph.D., is a Chicago-area therapist trained in Eagala Equine Assisted Psychotherapy. Asked to describe this modality of therapy, Linda says:

Basically, Equine Assisted Psychotherapy uses horses experientially for emotional and psychological learning and growth. It involves a treatment team made up of a licensed therapist, a horse professional, and a horse (or horses) to work with clients. It is considered a form of "brief" therapy because of its intensity and the number of sessions that are involved.

By experiential, we mean that clients learn about themselves and others by participating in activities with the horses. They then can process that experience and learning with the therapist and equine specialist. Much of its power comes from utilizing the living, breathing horse, a powerful symbol in and of itself. It is a dynamic interacting system.

Its focus is not riding therapy or horsemanship. It uses ground activities only. No riding. The activities emphasize such skills as non-verbal communication, creative problem solving, assertiveness, leadership, responsibility, teamwork, relationships, and attitude.

It is effective for a wide range of mental health issues, as well as personal growth, and team building. These include behavioral issues, attention deficit/ hyperactivity, anxiety, depression, abuse issues, addiction, relationship problems, and communication.

Horses are large and powerful making them naturally intimidating to many. This creates a natural opportunity for some to overcome fear and develop confidence. Working alongside a horse, in spite of those fears, creates confidence and provides wonderful insight when dealing with other intimidating and challenging situations in life.

Additionally, horses are social animals, with defined roles within their herds. They have distinct personalities, attitudes and moods; an approach that works with one horse won't necessarily work with another. At times, they seem stubborn and defiant, much like humans. They like to have fun as well. Horses provide vast opportunities for metaphorical learning, an effective technique when working with even the most challenging individuals or groups.

Horses are different than dogs. For instance, they are prey animals. As such, their very survival depends on picking up important clues from the environment and being able to *run to protect themselves. They naturally see us as a predator.*

Therefore, horses require us to work, whether in caring for them or working with them in a much different way than other animals. Horses require people to be engaged in physical and mental work to be successful, a valuable lesson in all aspects of life.

Most importantly, horses mirror human body language. A client may state, "This horse is stubborn. That horse doesn't like me," etc. The lesson is that if they change themselves, the horses respond differently. Horses are honest, which makes them especially powerful messengers.

I am currently working with a veteran who suffered a traumatic brain injury, leading to post traumatic stress disorder. Since we have begun the work with horses as part of his treatment team, he has been able to recall memories of events that for the past nineteen years have been locked away. We are hopeful that he will now be able to begin working through the trauma and regain a sense of safety and control in his everyday life.

The Animal Companion as Inner Child

Viewing human-animal interactions as I do through a therapist's lens, it seems to me that an animal companion, in some cases, becomes the representative of a person's inner child. If you have done or are doing your own work in therapy, or if you have read about how to heal psychic wounds suffered in childhood, you have probably worked on re-parenting that inner child within you. When I work with clients on this issue in therapy, I use various techniques: guided imagery, talk therapy, talking to or journaling with a childhood photo, among others.

Yet I notice that some of my clients who have bonded very deeply with an animal companion seem to see the animal as an externalized version of their own inner child. They give to that inner child/animal all the nurturing, validation, kindness and support that they should have received as children. In doing so, the people seem to grow in their confidence and self-esteem. Through their pet, they are healing their childhoods.

One example is Heather, a 54-year-old woman and her Yorkshire terrier mix, Polly. Heather grew up in a family that was at times abusive, and always unstable. When Heather became a single mother, she had difficulty parenting. To her sorrow, she repeated some of the same patterns she had grown up with. When Heather's son Tyler was seven years old, Heather adopted Polly. Heather took responsibility for the dog because her son was too young, and Heather found that she was able to care for Polly with more patience and kindness than she had been able to show Tyler. This caused her great shame, but she soon found that Polly's presence caused some mysterious and positive change in the family dynamic. After Polly's arrival, Heather began to treat her son with respect and caring.

"Polly brought out a gentleness in me. I was able to see how dependent she was on me, and how sweet she was. I wanted to make her happy and safe, and it was easy to do. I felt successful. I felt safe from failure with her."

Heather was able to access the nurturing aspect of her personality through the little dog. She had not been able to achieve this through her human child, she said, because human children are more demanding; Heather had been so depleted of emotional reserves through her painful childhood, she found it very difficult to be appropriately responsive to a child's demands. I asked

80

Heather if her child reminded her too much of her inner child that she was still rejecting at that time. Heather thought that might be so.

"Dogs demand nothing," said Heather. "They are happy with so little: a little kibble and a place to sleep. I could care for Polly on my own terms. I could nurture when I had it in me to nurture, and Polly would be happy with that." Heather grew her confidence in her ability to be nurturing.

Next, she was able to take a fresh look at how she had been taking out frustrations on her child, and make amends. Tyler has grown to be a well-adjusted and successful high school student. Heather has talked with him about her lack of parenting skills in the early years, and let him know that the issue was never about him, but about her own inability to deal with frustration. They have a good relationship now, and Heather is relieved that he seems to be emotionally healthy, as Heather says, "in spite of my mistakes." She is deeply regretful of those mistakes she made as a young parent. At the same time, she is mystified by the changes in self-development that her rescued Yorkie brought out in her.

"That little dog made me feel safe and strong," she marvels. "I could try new things. I felt like a capable adult because of her." My theory is that Heather's inner child felt safe, as Heather "parented" Polly, its outward representation.

We humans project all kinds of things onto those we love, without meaning to and without awareness. It's a beautiful thing when healing occurs, for whatever reason.

Part Three: Bonding

The Gift of the Bond

The Gift of the Bond

Life among Dogs

Teddy Bear, the Chihuahua – French bulldog mix, snores and makes grumbling and muttering noises as he slumbers. As we drift off to sleep, we hear him repeating what sound like short, thoughtful phrases. As we listen, they begin to sound like utterances. "Let me know. Let me know. Let me know." Or it may sound like: "Oh my, a magpie. Oh my, a magpie."

Every morning, Teddy Bear climbs out from under the covers of our bed to stretch his chestnut colored limbs and then give his head a good, vigorous shake. I always open my eyes at the sound of his metal tags tinkling together as he purposefully vibrates from head to toe. And that's when he draws his head back, ever so quickly, and sneezes, right in my eyes. That's how I start my day: just like so many other people, waking up with pets in the bed.

Teddy Bear, the Chihuahua-French bulldog rescue, now sometimes called "the fair-haired bear" by his loving family. Photo by Tom Davy.

The Pet Parent of Today

"The pet owner of today is very different from the pet owner of 15 years ago."

I heard this statement at the Illinois State Veterinary Medical Association Conference in 2014, and no one in the seminar disagreed. I know it to be true myself.

Fifteen years ago, you would not have heard anyone refer to his cat as "my son." You would not have heard the vet tech say to your dog, "Will Mom (referring to you, of course) let you have a treat?" The first time I ever heard anyone refer to her dog as her "soul mate" was only about five years ago, and it startled some people. Now these changes in the way we talk about our connections to our companion animals are no longer extraordinary. They have rapidly become part of the fabric of our culture, like so many other rapid changes.

There are changes occurring, subtly and not so subtly, in the way we think and talk about the creatures who share this planet with us. There are more vegetarians and vegans, there is more concern about puppy mills, factory farms and animal testing, and there is definitely more connection between people and their companion animals.

Are all of these changes in society somehow connected? I think they might be.

We long for connection as human beings always have, while at the same time being more isolated from one another than ever before. The internet and television give us the impression that we are having interactions, but they lack the warmth and eye-to-eye, soul-to-soul connection that are so life-giving. It's our dogs and cats (and ferrets, house rabbits, parrots and horses) that heal our hearts with their beating hearts and loving presence.

People are more stressed than ever before. We are nutritionally impoverished, sleep-deprived, frazzled from over-scheduling and trying to multi-task. The human beings we love may not be present for us, because they are on their smart phones. And we may not be present for them, because we are tweeting and posting.

Meanwhile, the cat curls herself into a perfect circle on our lap.

The dog settles in next to us, nuzzling our arm, leaning against our leg.

The animal is the only one who comes to find us in the blazing, buzzing, electronics-filled house. And we feel accompanied on our solitary path; we feel deeply loved; we love in return.

Of course we still love our people, too. But it's the companion animal who values us enough to give us warmth and time. This meets our very deep need for connection. We appreciate that. And so, we bond.

Are the connections between human and animal actually deeper than they used to be? Or have we as people always felt this quasi-parental or soul-connection to our pets, but only now, in the growing openness of our society, do we feel free and fearless enough to talk about it?

What Is This Love?

The connection we can have with our companion animals is so deep and multi-stranded. As I work with people who have had to say good-bye to this connection, I am touched by the eloquence of expression that the bereft find when describing that tie:

"He was my greatest support."

"Many boyfriends over the years have said to me, 'OK, it's me or the dog,' and I have always told them, 'It's been nice knowing you.'"

"No other animal can ever complete me the way Maisie did."

"Everyone in the neighborhood knew Jasper and me; we were always seen together; now I feel like I have to learn who I am without him."

"It's like I've lost a part of myself. It's somehow worse than when I've lost people that I loved. Now, how can that be?"

There are many reasons why this bond is so deep and so different from the other bonds in our life.

First, there is the aspect of physical touch. Many people touch their dog or cat far more than they touch any human being. Your pet may sit on your lap or rest his head on your feet while you work at the computer, watch TV, or read a book.

Second, there is the routine, every-day togetherness. When you get up to go to make breakfast, when you read a book on the couch, when you come in after running errands, there is your friend. You may take your pet for walks or car rides. You have a pattern of feeding, possibly medicating, and playing with your pet.

Third, if your bond was deep, you probably communicated regularly with your animal friend, verbally or non-verbally. You may have talked to your animal, and he may have seemed to understand you. "That dog understood every word I said, I truly believe that. I just talked to him and I could tell by the way he met my gaze, he was taking it all in." "My cat knew what I was feeling. She would come to me when I was sick or sad, and just give me her peaceful presence. She *knew*." When that source of communication, that feeling of being understood by another, is gone, it is a lonely feeling.

Fourth, our relationship with our pet is simple, even while being multi-stranded. It is simple because, unlike human relationships, it is completely clean of judgment, criticism, insincerity, deception—in short, it is free of all the negative complexities that we may experience with people. It is what it seems to be: pure love and devotion. That's why we prize it so much.

Fifth, and last, our animals depend upon us completely. Some people view their animals as their children. "They are like kids who never go through a disagreeable adolescence; they keep loving you and needing you, and they don't leave home." This dependence meets our instinctive need to nurture.

Considering all of these various ways of connection we have with our pets, it is only logical that we would feel pain and grief at the loss of that connection. Of course, not everyone is so deeply connected with their pets. But for those who have the privilege and joy to have such a profound bond with an animal friend, the loss of that friend can be devastating. While grief is normal, healthy and inevitable, there is always the concern that a deep grief could trigger a chronic depression. If you are reading this because you are grieving the passing of a dear animal friend, whether recent, long ago, or still anticipated, please do yourself the kindness to acknowledge the importance of your feelings, and allow yourself to seek support, either in a pet grief support group, or with an individual therapist whose focus is on pet grief.

And while I have referred to the "loss of the connection," I would like to invite you to consider that phrase and ask yourself if we do, in fact, lose the connection when our animal friend passes on. One way of coping with grief is to focus on how we have internalized the loved one, and in what ways he or she will always be a part of us. Some people believe that death does not end a relationship; that the relationship can continue evolving even after one of the partners has died. What is your experience, or your belief about the continuing connection between you and your dearest animal friend?

Unique Bond

In a wonderful book on Pet grief: *Saying Good-bye to the Pet You Love* by Lorri A. Greene, Ph.D. and Jacquelyn

Landis, the authors discuss why some people suffer profoundly on the loss of a pet, while others get a little misty-eyed for a moment and then move on. The answer is intuitive, and you already know it: the deeper the bond, the deeper the grief. However, what these authors add is a way of quantifying that bond. The book provides a quiz to help you understand if you are "conventionally bonded," "intensely bonded," or "uniquely bonded" to your animal friend.

Some people, of course, are not bonded at all with the pet. The dog is there to bark if a stranger comes; the cat is there to catch mice. The pets may be left outside a good deal of the time. An animal is an animal, and the non-bonded person really doesn't think much about the subject.

The "conventionally bonded" pet owner takes good care of the animal, exercising him, taking him to the vet as needed. They may refer to the animal as a "member of the family," but they do not give the animal the same status as a human member of the family. When the animal passes on, he may have some kind of a memorial ceremony, perhaps scattering the ashes in the yard, and tears may flow. Then, it's back to the demands of daily life, and the pet is remembered fondly.

The "intensely bonded" think of their pet as a full family member. They may prepare special food for their animal friend, and enjoy watching him or her eat. The pet may sleep with the person, and is involved in as many family activities as possible, probably even posing in the family photo. The intensely bonded suffer the loss of this relationship very deeply.

Those who are uniquely bonded think of their animal companion as their "little girl," their "son" or "daughter," or their "soul mate." In my practice and in my experience with pet grief groups, I have seen that this is often so. Some people even describe their pets as "part of their identity". I have seen some animal-human duos in which I felt that the animal might have represented the person's inner child, and was giving the person the opportunity to nurture that part of himself. The uniquely bonded person has the conviction that his animal understands him better than most people do. The person may prefer the company of his animal friend to that of many people, finding it consistently warm, comforting and supportive, unlike some human relationships. The uniquely bonded person will spare no expense when it comes to the medical care of his animal friend. When the time comes to say good-bye, the grief is so profound, that the person may have a very hard time recovering.

These three types of bonds which Greene describes provide a way of understanding why pet grief is so devastating for some people, and has only a minor effect on others.

You may find yourself grieving more deeply over one animal friend than another. No doubt you connected to one animal more deeply than another; perhaps also the depth of the grief had something to do with other issues in your life at the time; it's not only what the animal meant to you, but also what the circumstances of the death meant to you.

Please believe, your heart can heal. It may not seem like it ever will. You need a space to talk about your animal friend, to mourn without anyone trying to talk you out of that process, to acknowledge the significance of the loss.

Then there will eventually come a day when you remember your animal friend with more joy than sorrow.

Yes, but <u>Should</u> People Love Their Pets So Much?

I was having lunch with my accountant friend Sara, and the conversation turned to my work in pet grief counseling. She was very interested in learning about the unique bond that many people experience with their animal companions, and about how I help people through their grief when the animal passes away.

"Yes," she said, impatiently, "but, Joy, I have to ask myself: *should* people love their pets so much? I mean, shouldn't all that energy be going toward people and not animals? Yes, yes, I understand all about the 'unconditional love' and the animal is 'a member of the family'—but still: it's an *animal* member of the family. Isn't there something misplaced here? How do you help these people form connections with *humans*?"

My first reaction was amusement at the human need to judge and to change anything that is not immediately understood. So unlike a dog or a cat, I thought. Animals teach us to stay with curiosity a little longer, before judging. Animals also teach us that if we are not being directly threatened, we can skip judging and choose to go straight to acceptance, even if we do not understand.

"Well, Sara," I said thoughtfully, "I don't see it as my role as a counselor to assist people to not feel what they feel, or to love differently. If a person has a strong connection to an animal companion, there is a reason for that, and that connection is beautiful and to be honored. In fact, a big part of my work is to help people to *not* judge their own feelings—but just to sit with them, be curious about them, and observe."

Sara has been noticing that her aunt is suffering a prolonged grief after the death of her schnauzer. Part of Sara's impatience with pet grief is that she does not want to see her aunt suffer. She loves her aunt and would like to see her recover, move on, be happy and engaged in life as she was before. So part of Sara's way of coping with her own discomfort in the face of pet grief is to judge it as invalid or somehow "wrong." Standing in that position, she can distance herself from her aunt's pain by seeing her grief as "misplaced," or "inappropriate."

I have noticed that people who find a great deal of emotional support in an animal companion may have been deeply hurt by a person, or people in general, in the past. In some cases, the animal is emotionally available and loving in a way that people may not always be. However, my observation has also been that people who do have this unique bond with an animal do also have human connections. They are not isolated with their animal companion, shut off from human contact. They generally do have friends and loving connections with family. Each relationship, human and animal, meets some need, provides some comfort or support. Each relationship, whether with humans or animals, is unique. It is a spirit-to-spirit connection.

Sara's question, "*Should* people love their pets so much?" is an interesting one. It inspires other questions: Why do we love the beings we love? Should we love anyone at all? What is the point of loving others? How does it benefit us to love? How does it benefit the world if we love?

Accompanying people through pet grief, I feel honored and deeply conscious of the privilege of being allowed to bear witness to the beautiful and deep connections between beings. The grief is, in a way, beautiful because it acknowledges deep love.

We love because we cannot do otherwise. We were born to love. "Shoulds" do not enter into it.

Pets that Complete a Family

A beloved pet can provide a sense of "family." The animal gives a focus for attention and love, and gives the feeling of being needed. For empty nesters and for those who have never had children, an animal can fulfill that instinct to nurture that most of us have.

Companion animals have the dependency of small children that never grow up, and never go through a teenage rebellion. You need to feed them, keep them safe and sheltered, give them medical attention and affection. Like small children, they give you unchanging love and admiration. They never question that you are the center of their universe.

Just as parents see themselves as linked in their identity to their children, as a pet owner you may see yourself linked to your animal. The veterinarian's receptionist may call you "Taffy's mom" or "Junior's dad." Your neighbors, friends, extended family and co-workers may come to know you as a duo. It's not just a link that you see, it is a link that others see, a link that the animal feels, a link that is very real.

Barb has shared her home with cats for most of her life, beginning when a black kitten, Mimi, was given to her family many years ago. Each successive cat lived a long and comfortable life, eventually joined by a younger companion who comforted Barb in her grief when each cat in her turn reached the end of her life. All the cats have been rescued black females, and Barb gave them all

93

names that started with the letter "M": Mimi shared the second half of her life with Marla; then Marla was the only cat for a short time before being joined by Maeve. When Marla passed, Barb was living with her mother, and they together adopted Majesty to keep Maeve company. As both Maeve and Majesty reached their senior years, Barb and her mother opened their home to a black kitten, Mona. Eventually, Maeve and Majesty passed, and Mona enjoyed all the attention to herself.

When Barb's mother died, Barb grieved deeply. Her relationship with her mother had been complicated, as human relationships tend to be, but since her divorce many years before, Barb and her mother had shared their home, their lives, and their cats. Mona seemed to understand Barb's sorrow, and became more affectionate, cuddling close to Barb's face, "combing" Barb's hair with her claws, and purring. Mona was a young cat, and Barb believed that she would be her last cat, and that she and Mona would become "little old ladies together."

"Mona used to sit with me while I read in the living room. She had a perch on the wide window sill of the picture window, where she could watch the squirrels and birds. Whenever a chipmunk would go running along the outside window ledge, Mona would chirp in this special way she had, just for chipmunks. She had different little trills and chirps for telling me she was hungry, and for telling me she loved me."

Barb had the very clear impression that Mona understood Barb's words and thoughts, and she felt that she also understood Mona's inner world to a great extent, and was always trying to understand her more. The connection between them was very strong.

Tragedy struck, however, when at the age of five, Mona became ill very suddenly. She died of feline pancreatitis, which Barb's vet said was very unusual for such a young cat. The death was shocking, unlike the deaths of all the other cats, who had died in old age after a brief illness. Mona was playing and running one day, and gone the next. Barb was in disbelief.

Barb's vet, Dr. James, who had known her through all the cats, was deeply saddened by this unexpected death. He liked Barb and had developed a relationship with her over the years, and he and his staff had loved Mona: she had had a "big personality."

"Go out and get yourself another black kitten right away; do not wait," Dr. James counseled.

Generally, it's best if grieving people follow their own time frame on getting another pet. Telling someone who is in shock and grief to "get another one" can imply that animal companions are replaceable, like material objects, which they definitely are not. And generally, it works best to have some time to grieve first, before bringing a new animal into one's life. Adopting another animal too soon may result in a person making unfair comparisons between the pet who has died and the new one, and in taking out his or her grief on the unsuspecting and innocent new pet. The person may find it very difficult to bond with the new animal, and even resent him or her, wishing that this animal could be gone, and that the one who has passed on could be here instead.

Dr. James is aware of the reasons not to tell people to immediately "get another one," but in this case, he was intentionally not following the general rule.

"Barb lives alone. She is still grieving the death of her mother. This grief on top of that one will be too much for her, I am afraid. She has always been so wrapped up in her cats, so attentive to them, and they have made her so happy. I cannot imagine Barb, all alone, without a cat to love and care for."

Barb has a rich and full social life, and many cherished friendships that are "just like family to me." Living alone had never bothered her before, because she had all the social life she wanted, and she shared her quiet times at home with Mona. But, she says, going into her house after Mona died was an awful experience.

"Our lovely new home that I bought for Mona and me, and that I decorated for us, the house where Mona and I would grow to be two old ladies together, is now a *dead house*, and I hate it," said Barb, weeping.

A friend searched local rescue groups online and soon found a black, female kitten who needed a home. Barb adopted her gratefully, and with immense relief, brought "Mona Marie" home.

"People told me not to give the new cat the same name, but it's not the same name, really: my Mona, who I will always love, and this new little one, Mona Marie. That's what I'm naming her, whatever anyone says."

Mona Marie instantly took away the "dead house feeling." Scampering madly about, creating all kinds of new-kitten mischief, despite her tiny size, she filled the house with life and activity. Although Barb was still deep in her grief, she now had someone to attend to, and she had companionship at home.

However, she did find herself frustrated and annoyed with this kitten, who, apart from appearance, had nothing at all in common with Mona.

"Mona was a calmer cat. Even as a kitten, I don't think she was this wild and crazy. *My* Mona never climbed the curtains, never used her claws on me or bit me when I pet her. This Mona Marie is a devil child!" Barb gave a short laugh, and then sighed, shaking her head.

"Mona was sensitive, spiritual, yet with an assertive and loving personality, commanding attention, but in a sweet way. This one is brash, obnoxious, and nutty."

"I just want *my* Mona back. I tell Mona Marie every day, 'You're a cute little girl, yes you are, but you're not my Mona. If I could have my Mona back, I would trade you away in a New York minute, yes I would.'" Before Barb could finish this speech, Mona Marie, ears back, tore wildly out of the room, like a squad car chasing bad guys down the highway.

Even a year and a half later, Barb was deeply mourning Mona. She took impeccable care of Mona Marie, but she did not love her as deeply as she loved Mona, and wondered if she ever would. The original Mona was a link to Barb's mother, and Barb considered that when Mona went, some living link to Barb's life with her mother went with her. Mona Marie did not seem connected to the chain of black cats that were part of the family life Barb shared with her mother.

Did Barb make a mistake in adopting a kitten too soon after the shocking and sudden death of the cat she adored? She wondered sometimes. Perhaps it's not as simple as making or not making "a mistake." Mona Marie has presented two things to Barb: relief from the "dead house" feeling; and frustration that Mona Marie is not Mona.

In our sessions, Barb came to consider how Mona Marie might be receiving this message of "I don't love you" from Barb. We are always wondering how our animals perceive things, and how it is that they sometimes seem to understand things that should be beyond their grasp. Of course, Mona Marie did not understand Barb's words in plain English. But could she sense Barb's rejection?

"I would hate to think she would feel that from me," said Barb. "She doesn't deserve it. But what can I do?"

Barb realized that one reason she was not opening her heart to Mona Marie was the fear of being disloyal to her original Mona. Barb did believe that Mona had sent the new kitten to her, to comfort her. From there, Barb was able to make the connection that she should receive this parting gift from Mona with gratitude.

Next, Barb decided to adopt the "act as if" approach: speaking gently and with endearments to the new kitten, and reassuring the little newcomer that she was safe, welcomed, and loved for her own self.

Barb and Mona are settling into their new relationship. No animal ever replaces another, any more than one person replaces another. But Barb is deeply comforted by this energetic and spunky young cat, and she is forming a new and equally unique love.

Mary and Ed are a couple in their late sixties, with one adult son who has grown very distant from them since his return from Iraq. Before he left, their relationship had been warm, but since his return, he has had a personality change, and is angry with everyone, especially his parents. Mary and Ed know he has been diagnosed with PTSD and is using substances, but he does not let them get close enough to understand more or to offer help. Mary, an immigrant from Korea, has no family here other than her son, husband and dogs. Mary and Ed have always been a harmonious couple, and shared their home with two retriever mixes, Carmen and Butterfly, named after opera heroines.

Mary and Ed worked hard every day and came home to their dogs, who did "the happy dance" for them every evening. When they were at home, Mary and Ed centered their routines and activities around Carmen and Butterfly. Walks, car rides, visits with friends: Carmen and Butterfly were always involved, wagging their bushy tails and lavishing love and appreciation on Mary, Ed, and everyone they ever met.

Carmen and Butterfly unified Mary and Ed as they went through the challenges and changes that life brought them. The dogs gave a sense of family to their household. As Mary and Ed worried about their grown son and grieved the loss of connection with him, the dogs, while not "making up for" that loss, did provide comfort, reassurance, and a different kind of connection.

When Butterfly became fatally ill, and the vet told Mary and Ed that Butterfly was suffering with no options for recovery, they felt a heavier sense of grief than they had ever felt before.

Mary came to the pet grief support group, while Ed, although in just as deep grief, chose not to come with her. He told her that he does "not want to get upset in front of other people." Mary reached out for help because she was overwhelmed with her sadness, and knew she needed help and support to bear this pain. Her eyes overflowed with tears and she found it hard to speak. She told how Butterfly was diagnosed with cancer and very soon after, Mary and Ed were faced with the decision to euthanize, or to allow Butterfly to suffer an agonizing death.

"We were in shock. How could this happen so fast? Our other dog, Carmen, has cancer, too, and we have been giving her medicine and a special diet for ten months. Carmen is doing well. I know she still has cancer, but right now she has a good life. In my mind, I was getting ready to let Carmen go. Not Butterfly. Butterfly was healthy. That's what we thought. I can't believe this happened."

Mary and Ed spent most of their savings trying one thing and another, conventional and alternative, to save Butterfly, finding it impossible to believe that she was to be "taken" from them so soon. Finally, when nothing worked, they agreed to euthanasia. Even though it was very clearly the only humane option left, they felt enormous guilt, as many pet owners do.

Now, while grieving the death of one cherished animal friend, Mary and Ed have the heavy emotional task of continuing to prepare for the death of the other. They will benefit from emotional support through the challenges to come.

The Sibling Pet

David Remkus, at the Hinsdale Animal Cemetery, first brought to my conscious attention the concept of the "sibling pet." This is a child's pet who fills the role of a supportive and always-available sibling. Many times, this relationship develops between an animal and an only child. Sometimes, there are human siblings, but in any case, the animal meets a deep need for connection in the child. There seems to be a profound understanding between them. The animal prefers this child to the other people in the family, and the child rushes home from school with happiness in his or her heart, knowing that "Lulu" or "Rowdy" will be at the door, joyful at their reunion.

I personally experienced the dynamic of the sibling pet. This was the closest bond I ever had with any animal previously or subsequently, although I have loved animals all my life, and continue to share my life with them. Sandy, however, was that once-in-a-lifetime connection for me.

Sandy was a blond cocker spaniel puppy that my mother found through an ad in the paper. I had been pleading for a dog of my own for two years, leaving notes, signs, and illustrated reminders all over the house, telling my parents that unlike other children, I really would take responsibility for *my* dog.

Finally, on a June day in 1967, just before I turned ten, we drove out to the country to see the advertised litter of puppies in a fenced enclosure in a rural back yard. I remember this more vividly than anything else in my childhood. It was early evening, unseasonably cool, a light breeze blowing. The yellow puppies were spilling madly all over each other. I was enchanted. In my mind's eye, I can see my dad, wearing his light spring jacket. He squatted down and tapped on the ground, and all the puppies came tumbling over each other to get to him. He picked up one, a female, and my mother, standing, said, "No, not a female." He picked up another one who immediately licked his ear. My father made the decision then: "This is the one," he declared. My mother, concurred, "Yes, a male."

I'm not sure why it was important to her to get a male that day; perhaps it was the thinking of the day that it's better to have a male because they don't have litters. Remember, it was the sixties, and people weren't as conscientious about spaying and neutering as they are now.

I recall the ride home, with my mother holding the puppy in the front seat. I asked once if I could hold him, and she said no. I didn't argue. I had my dog!

My mother named him Sandy, because, she said, his fur was the color of sand.

To my parents' surprise, I did take responsibility for Sandy: feeding, walking, brushing and playing with him. We had just moved to a new town. I had no siblings and no friends. Sandy rapidly became my everything.

Because I was his source of food, fun and attention, he bonded to me, and because he was my long-awaited canine friend, I bonded to him. I loved everything about that dog: the way he slept with his hind legs stretched out behind him in front of the fireplace, the wavy golden hair on his ears, and his responsiveness to everything I taught him. I would take him to the schoolyard nearby to play, and I could let him off leash; he would always come scampering back as soon as I whistled. Just that alone exhilarated me.

When the new school year began, I was anxious and nervous, knowing no one in this new place, but in the afternoons, when I walked home, there Sandy would be, looking out from behind the screen door, wagging his tail and going mad with delight. For the rest of the afternoon and evening, he would fill my heart with love and confidence. After a move (in a succession of far too many moves) that left me feeling that I had no place where I belonged and no long-term friendships, I now had a friend who would be with me for years to come, my very own best friend. It wouldn't be going too far to say: I was obsessed with my dog.

Sandy, like most dogs will do unless taught otherwise, barked at strangers passing in front of the house and at unfamiliar noises.

My father was a very anxious man, easily upset and easily angered. Loud noises shattered his nerves. As a child, I did not understand, that at that time, he was on the brink of what they used to call "a nervous breakdown." Sandy's barking set my dad yelling and covering his ears, and declaring that the dog had to go, he couldn't stand that noise any more.

In these comparatively enlightened times, we know that squirting a dog with a water bottle, and at the same time saying, "Quiet," will train a dog to pipe down, eventually just responding to the mere word, "quiet." But in the sixties, people didn't know much about training dogs. If there was a problem you couldn't figure out how to solve, you "got rid of him." You "put an ad in the paper."

My father spoke with his psychologist about this problem: the now 11-year-old daughter who was deeply attached to the cocker spaniel, the irritating, unbearable noise the dog made, and my father's desperation to get the animal out of his house.

My father's psychologist, an avuncular, sad-eyed man called Dr. Jaznow, warned my dad to find a way to keep the dog. He advised that this dog was "the child's emotional support through a difficult transition," and much more than "just a dog" as my father saw him. He predicted that "getting rid of the dog" would plunge me into grief and adversely affect the relationship between my father and me in the long term. Dr. Jaznow's prediction proved to be correct.

My father had a nervous collapse which he blamed on Sandy, and on my uncaring insistence on keeping a dog that barked and made him so nervous. My heartless lack of concern for how the dog was making him sick, he said, was the reason he had fallen to pieces and couldn't get out of bed. It was all my selfish fault. At his urging, my mother put an ad in the paper to sell Sandy.

I remember the man who came to the door. He seemed very kind, and truly sorry for the child that I was, crying in the living room. My mother had Sandy on the leash, and handed it to this stranger, who hesitated, looking at me, and then wrote his name, phone number and address in block letters, saying that he lived on a farm where Sandy would have lots of room to run and other dogs to play with, and we could come and visit him any time. That slip of paper sat under the candy dish on the coffee table for many months. We never did go.

To know that Sandy was happy somewhere else should have been a comfort, but I was only a child, and I was not comforted. I only desperately wanted him back.

As an eleven year old, I did not understand anything about nervous collapses. Self-centered as any other child, I only knew that when Sandy left, most of my life force seemed to go with him. I cried, and was told to stop being silly, so I cried privately, every day, for more than a year. My relationship with my father was strained and difficult from that point on.

Now, grown and trained in psychotherapy myself, I am better able to understand my father's pain, and I can now see how he struggled with this decision, how guilty he felt, and how helpless he was in the face of his psychiatric symptoms. I forgive him with all my heart, and love and appreciate his memory. He was a good man, struggling with mental illness.

I can also look back with compassion at my own pet grief, and understand that I was not selfish, silly or stubborn. I bonded deeply, as we are designed to do, and I resisted letting go of that healing bond, as we all tend to do.

That experience with loving and losing Sandy, more than any other, is what helps me understand pet grief in my work today. As I accompany others on their grief path, I am healed from that long-ago loss of my sibling-pet.

Old Dog with Purpose

This is a piece I wrote about Jules, my first canine co-therapist. I include it here, because it is an example of how one person connects with an animal companion, my human perspective on my canine friend and the bond we share through working and living together.

Dr. Jules, my co-therapist of the canine persuasion, continues to make appearances at my office. His heart pounds so during the car ride, I'm not sure if it's in his best interest to go. But once his curly poodle ears hear "going to work," he hobbles to the door and stands at the ready, wanting me to pick him up and take him along.

His clients need him, he tells me.

Some days, it's all he can do to give a good greeting to our clients, before a deep nap overtakes him.

Today, he was at the top of his game, making a major fuss at each client's entrance, vocalizing with chimpanzee-like noises, his little stick-tail wagging like a metronome gone ballistic, making his people laugh.

Then, as we sit down to talk, he settles down with mature dignity at his client's feet, with his back toward his client in that stance that means "trust" in the dog world, and he makes no more fuss, allowing the humans to talk, sensing that his participation in the conversation is on pause for now.

At times he stretches out on the carpet, arching his back and reaching in both directions with his front and back paws, as if saying, "If you're talking about relaxation techniques, check this out."

And then he falls asleep.

Maybe his nap demonstration is therapeutic, too. Or maybe he is ready to retire?

But when his client rises to leave, Jules is up and involved again, wagging his tail, making his quiet little fuss. "You're wonderful," he says. "Please stay. Please come back soon. Take my blessing with you. You're wonderful."

Jules teaches me a lot about life: facing challenges (he is blind), ageing with grace (when I adopted him they said he was 10 years old, but that was just a guess), dealing with rejection (the Chihuahua club at my house tolerates him icily; he doesn't get to be in their mutual face-washing parties, but they wouldn't be so unkind as to ever growl at him, either).

Jules sits outside, soaking in the sun's rays, closing his blind eyes, feeling the breeze ruffle his silky poodle hair.

He stretches out, with his feet straight back behind him, and enjoys a quick nap. He gets up and runs around the yard, now that he has mapped out where the trees and fence are, and he runs with his floppy ears flapping, barking for the fun of it. Just one little peppy sprint, and that's enough for him.

He barks assertively--and surprisingly loudly-- when he finds himself alone: "What the heck? Where's the party? Helloooo?" And we have to go upstairs or downstairs to get him, and bring him to where we are. Then he settles in for a nice rest, as long as he can hear our voices near, and get a nice gentle neck massage.

He walks along confidently at the end of a leash, trusting life, even though he can't see what's ahead.

Whatever he does, he is in the moment, enjoying himself, giving love to whoever is open to receive it.

I think he is my role model.

People make a mistake when they overlook the senior dogs as potential adoptees. An old dog demands so little, is content just to be alive and be near his or her people. If we all required so little from life, we'd all be as happy every day as Jules is.

Jules, a blind senior therapy dog, full of the joie de vivre

Strengthening the Bond with Your Pet

Creating a stronger bond with a pet usually tends to be an easy and natural thing. Sometimes, however, there can be a block in the way of the bond. For example, feral cats who were not socialized during the critical period of their kitten-hood may take a very long time and a lot of patience on the part of their people to bond—if they ever do; the bond will most likely look very different from the bond that the people would like to have. A dog who was mistreated and who has learned to bite people will have a long road to go, and will need to work with an experienced and gentle trainer. And a person who has been through deep grief after the loss of a pet, and who is now bringing a new animal companion on board, may also present a block to the bonding, without even realizing it.

If you are working on the bond with a new pet after (or during) pet grief, it will be important for you to release any notion that loving this new pet is an act of disloyalty to the deceased pet. Reflect on this: our pets' lives are shorter than ours. They were never meant to accompany us the whole length of our road here—only a certain part of the way. The love you have for the deceased pet will not decrease, and you will not forget. Just as the departed animal celebrated the small things and enjoyed life every day, that animal invites you, by example, to do the same. Hold the old love in your heart, and "pay it forward."

Here are some suggestions for strengthening the bond with your new friend:

- Be calm, consistent and reliable.
- Get on the same level with your cat or rabbit sometimes.
- Spend time: grooming, focused attention, talking.
- For cats and dogs, provide puzzles and games (such as hiding the treat under the blanket, etc.)
- With dogs, be outdoors as much as possible. Being out in the sun and fresh air will do you both good.
- Massage your pet, gently, with attention, in the way that your pet likes. Take the time to learn what makes your pet feel good.
- Hand-feeding is a good bonding activity to do once in a while.
- For cats, the famous "head bump" is a connection-builder: present your fist to the cat's nose; let him smell and rub his head against your hand. Do that a couple of times before petting him.

109

- Say kind and affectionate things to your pet. She may not understand "the King's English," but she completely understands your "vibe." You, meanwhile, do understand the words you are saying, and they help you to feel the connection you want to feel towards your new pet.
- While holding your pet, focus for a few seconds on the gratitude in your heart—for this particular animal, and for all animals, everywhere.

Sometimes bonding seems to be like love at first sight: instantaneous, and then building from there. In other relationships, bonding may have to begin from a depleted and grieving heart, and we may need to focus purposefully on opening our heart, gradually and with intention and deep thankfulness.

Making the Connection: Arriving at Animal Consciousness

Note: This chapter has been included for people who would like to consider vegetarianism or veganism as a path of compassion for animals. If this is not a path you are ready to consider, feel free to skip to the final pages where you will find "Parting Thoughts."

"We have to understand that we are not the only beings on this planet with personalities and minds."—Jane Goodall

Sheep at Farm Sanctuary in Watkins Glen, New York. Sheep are known to recognize different human faces and to remember them for years. Photo by Claire Smolinski.

When I was at a veterinary conference, some of the seminars offered were on "pet animals versus food animals." I attended a portion of one of these, in which the discussion was about treating cattle more humanely before slaughtering them for human consumption. As the slides depicting the "enlightened" and "humane" treatment were shown, I found I needed to leave the room, because the detailed discussion of how animals are treated in the most humane of slaughtering practices did not comfort me, but troubled me so deeply that I could not bear to hear or watch.

The question or challenge I put to you is: what, in your own heart, do you feel is the difference between "pet animals" and "food animals"? Do cows, pigs, sheep, turkeys and chickens feel fear? Do they feel pain? Do they think? Do they love? Do they bond?

Once you have deeply bonded with an animal, be it a beagle, a parrot, or a Siamese cat, you have been changed. It's not that you think your dog, for example, is not a dog but rather a person. We may joke that our "fur-babies" are "little people in fur coats", but if we are in our right minds, we understand that an animal is not a person. And yet, to us, our cherished animal friend is *not less* than a person. As a matter of fact, for you, your pet may be actually a better individual than most people you could name. You have, thanks to your animal, arrived at "animal consciousness." You are aware that your animal companion has feelings and thoughts; your pet is a true individual; he or she bonds deeply, is capable of feeling comfort, delight, love, curiosity, sadness, confusion and terror.

The next logical step is to consider: how is a pig different from a dog? Pigs are actually said to be more intelligent than dogs. They are deeply individual, just like our dogs

112

and cats, with their own personalities, likes and dislikes. Pigs can learn their names and come when they are called. They show affection, when living in an environment that allows it, to other pigs and to human caretakers. Pigs form lifelong, loving relationships with each other when in an environment that gives them the opportunity. We may feel horror to think of people in other parts of the world eating dogs; what do we feel, if we allow ourselves to feel it, about eating pigs?

Consider the cow. According to research by Dr. Alain Boissy and his colleagues at INRA: Institut National de la Récherche Agronomique (National Institute of Agricultural Research in Paris) which is quoted in *The Inner World of Farm Animals* by Amy Hatkoff, cows are empathic with one another. Cows take longer to learn a new task if they are in the company of a cow that is upset. Cows also seem to lose their appetites when their friends are under stress. The natural behavior for cows is to work together in a social way, "babysitting" for each other's calves, and grooming one another. Cows are very maternal, and love their offspring deeply, mourning when separated from their young—sometimes to the point of breaking down fences to get to their calves. Calves bawl for their mothers when taken from them.

The author, welcomed to Farm Sanctuary in Watkins Glen, New York, by a gentle giant of a cow, trusting and open to making a new friend. Photo by Claire Smolinski.

Chickens are also more intelligent than we realize, capable of learning from their mothers and other chickens through observation. They also mourn the loss of relationships, as do pigs, horses, cows, goats, and sheep.

Our "pet animals" are ambassadors to us from all the animals of the earth.

A goat at Farm Sanctuary in Watkins Glen, New York. Goats, like dogs, seek human affection, approaching people and rubbing against their legs. Photo by Claire Smolinski.

Parting Thoughts

"Until one has loved an animal, a part of one's soul remains unawakened."—Anatole France

You are one of the fortunate people whose soul has been awakened by the love you have had for an animal. Sadly, with love, come loss and grief. Also with love, comes healing. The love remains with you, and brings healing again, in time.

With our animal companions, we bond, we grieve, and we heal...and bond again.

Resources:

Be sure to avail yourself of the growing number of resources that exist for pet grief. Here are some good places to start.

Websites:

www.pet-loss.net Here you will find support groups (by clicking on your state on a map), hotlines, individual counselors, and helpful articles.

www.petloss.com This website has a pet grief chat room and articles on pet grief.

www.aspca.org/pet-care/pet-loss The American Society for the Prevention of Cruelty to Animals

www.vet.purdue.edu/chab This is the website for the Center for the Human-Animal Bond at Purdue University.

www.eagala.org Equine Assisted Growth and Learning Association: using equine therapy to address mental health and human development needs.

www.bestfriends.org This is an innovative no-kill sanctuary in Utah, caring for dogs, cats, rabbits, horses, and many other animals. It is a beautiful place to visit.

www.farmsanctuary.org There is one sanctuary in rural New York and another in California. Farm Sanctuary provides a safe and comfortable environment for farm animals to live out their days. When you visit, you will see happy cows, sheep, goats, turkeys, chickens and pigs living naturally. This is a good place to observe the intelligence and bonding behaviors of farm animals.

Hotlines:

1-866-266-8635. Washington State University. Veterinary medicine students trained in grief counseling by a licensed therapist.

1-630-325-1600. Pet Loss Helpline, Chicago Veterinary Medical Association.

http://www.pet-loss.net/resources/ At this website, you can search by state for a pet grief hotline.

Further Reading:

Coping with Sorrow on the Loss of Your Pet, by Moira Anderson Allen, M.Ed.

Goodbye, Friend: Healing Wisdom for Anyone Who Has Ever Lost a Pet, by Gary Kowalski

The Inner World of Farm Animals: Their Amazing Social, Emotional, and Intellectual Capacities, by Amy Hatkoff

The Power of Joy in Giving to Animals, by Linda Harper, Ph.D.

Saying Good-bye to the Pet You Love: A Complete Resource to Help You Heal, by Lorri A. Greene, Ph.D. and Jacquelyn Landis

The Souls of Animals, by Gary Kowalski

Acknowledgements:

My heart overflows with gratitude to the readers of my early manuscript, Dr. Linda Harper, PhD, and Claire Smolinski, who made meticulous notes of suggestions to improve the final draft of this book. Thank you also to Maura Vivona for your encouragement. I am deeply indebted also to David Remkus and Dr. Lori Coughlin, DVM, sources of knowledge and specialized experience.

48585156R00068

Made in the USA
Lexington, KY
06 January 2016